Guelphs & Ghibellines : a short history of mediaeval Italy from 1250-1409

Oscar Browning

UNIVERSITY EXTENSION SERIES

EDITED BY J. E. SYMES, M.A.
Principal of University College, Nottingham.

GUELPHS AND GHIBELLINES

29101

GUELPHS & GHIBELLINES

A SHORT HISTORY

OF

MEDIÆVAL ITALY FROM 1250-1409

Gen Hist

BY

OSCAR BROWNING

𝔐𝔢𝔱𝔥𝔲𝔢𝔫 & 𝔠𝔬.
18 BURY STREET, LONDON, W.C.
1894

FORTI NON DEFICIT TELUM

John Watts de Peyster.

To the Memory

OF

MY FRIEND

JOHN ADDINGTON SYMONDS

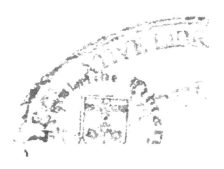

CONTENTS

CHAPTER I.

CHAPTER VIII.

CHAPTER IX.

CHAPTER X.

CHAPTER XI.

CHAPTER XII.

CHAPTER XIII.

CHAPTER XIV.

CHAPTER XV.

CONTENTS

GUELPHS AND GHIBELLINES.

CHAPTER I.

INTRODUCTION—FREDERICK BARBAROSSA—INNOCENT III.—
FREDERICK II.

By those who divide the whole of history into three great
periods, mediæval history is held to begin with the year 476
A.D., the year which witnessed the fall of the Empire of the
West. Whatever may have been the effect of this event
upon the world at large, it was certainly a great crisis in
the history of Italy. Romulus Augustulus, a Roman or a
Pannonian by birth, whose name recalled, by a curious
coincidence, the mythical origin and the constitutional
establishment of the Roman Empire, was deposed from
the imperial throne, and the Scyrrian Odoacer assumed
the title of King of Italy. He reigned from 476 to 493.
The year 489 marks the descent, into the Italian plains, of
the Ostrogoths, the Eastern division of the great Gothic
nation whose Western brethren conquered Spain and part
of Africa. Their first king was the mighty Theodoric, whose
palace still exists at Ravenna, and whose reign, immor-
talized in the earliest epics of the Teutonic race, extended
over the first quarter of the sixth century (489-526). For
twenty-five years longer his successors feebly maintained
the glory of the Gothic name, until in 553 they were unable

A

to withstand the power of the Emperor Justinian. This
famous law-giver was by origin a Slav, as his name, Uprada,
shows, so that the Ostrogoths were barbarians conquered
by a barbarian. In 568 a more powerful race descended
into the valley of the Po, the Lombards, or Longobardi,
under their king Alboin. Their dominion lasted for more
than two centuries, until the year 774. Italy was under
them divided into thirty-six duchies. There was a
Lombardy of the South around Beneventum, as there
was a Lombardy of the North around Milan. The latter
district has retained its name until our own day. We find
in these changes conditions which have been repeated
through succeeding ages until our own time. A German
race subjugates the rich territory of the South ; the popes,
the bishops of Rome, preserve their independence, and
become, in a certain sense, the asserters of Italian freedom.
Too weak to stand by their own power, the popes apply
for assistance to France. The arms of Pepin and of
Charlemagne supported the temporal power, as it was
afterwards supported by Charles of Anjou, by Charles of
Valois, by Charles VIII., and Napoleon III.

In 800 Charles the Great became Emperor of the West.
Lombardy was held by his family from its conquest in 774
till the expulsion of Charles the Fat in 888. The anarchy
which succeeded opened up Italy as a prey to new invaders.
The Hungarians poured down in a torrent from the North ;
the Saracens, who had conquered Sicily in the second
quarter of the century, pressed upwards from the South ;
while other swarms of the same race settled on the shores
of the Mediterranean between Genoa and Nice. These
horrors had one good result. The towns fortified themselves in self-defence, and with the help of their local

trained bands, laid the germs of future liberty. In 960 the Saxon Otho assumed the imperial crown of Charles the Great.

It is no part of the object of this book to describe in detail the early history of Mediæval Italy. The period with which we are concerned begins in 1250, after the death of the Emperor Frederick II., the last great monarch who founded a kingdom of Italy which was able to hold its own against the power of the popes. At the same time, it is necessary to trace, in their previous development, the forces which are found in full operation at the time when our narrative begins. We shall see, in the first place, a continual struggle going on between the power of the Emperor and the freedom of the towns. This had its origin from the establishment of a feudal hierarchy in Italy by Otho the Saxon, which was weak in power and short in duration. It scarcely lasted till the death of Otho III. in 1002. Conrad the Salian was not able to revive it, and we find at his death, in 1039, that the best protection for the security of the feudal princes lay in recommending themselves to the growing power of the towns. Another condition which affects the whole course of mediæval Italian history, is the constant contentions between the emperors and the popes. The relations between them began in the exchange of mutual benefits. The popes gave a divine sanction to the claim of the princes of the house of Charles the Great to bear the title of emperor, and received in return the recognition of their temporal sovereignty. A succession of weak and vicious popes failed to assert their power against the rival efforts of good and judicious emperors. The quarrel between them burst into flame when the boy Henry IV. was left to wield the sceptre of his grandfather Conrad, and when the mighty Hildebrand swayed the counsels of the Roman *curia*. Hildebrand, who governed each succeeding pope long before he assumed the tiara for himself, may be regarded as the founder of the papal power as it now exists. He insisted on the celibacy of the clergy, the first condition necessary for a devoted and obedient hierarchy, and at the council of the Lateran held in 1075, forbad all priests to receive investiture at the hands of laymen. This branded with illegality a feudal custom which had been regarded as usual in the confirmation of a prelate, and began a dispute which lasted throughout the middle ages, and can hardly even now be considered as extinct. Also by insisting on the importance of the doctrine of the real presence in the Eucharist, he tightened the band of intellectual submission to the authority of Rome. Having thus laid down a firm basis for his spiritual power, he obtained, by his alliance with the Countess Matilda of Tuscany, a better right than the pope had yet acquired to large material possessions. The seal was set to the efforts of a long career, when the Emperor Henry IV., clad in the shirt of penitence, stood with bare feet throughout three winter days in the courtyard of the castle of Canossa, and sued in vain for pardon. The rivalry between pope and emperor eventually took the form of civil war between Guelfs and Ghibellines.

The eleventh century witnessed the introduction of a new element into the quarrels of the Peninsula. The Normans, a Scandinavian race, who had brought a new language and a new civilisation into one of the fairest parts of France, began to found an empire in Italy, about fifty years before they accomplished the conquest of England. They overran

Apulia and Calabria, notwithstanding the resistance of the
popes, and proceeded to wrest Sicily from the hands of the
Saracens. They destroyed three centres of independence
which shone conspicuously on that portion of the Mediterranean coast which has too often been the seat of
tyranny and oppression—the republics of Naples, Gaeta, and
Amalfi, the last of which demands our special reverence.
The traveller who visits the little fishing town, squeezed in
between the mountains and the sea, affording a mere niche
of vantage on the iron-bound coast between the great
harbours of Palermo and Naples, finds it difficult to imagine
that he sees the site of a republic, which probably invented
the mariner's compass, which was among the first to give
laws to the commerce of the sea, and which preserved with
superstitious reverence the sacred copy of the pandects,
from which the knowledge of the Roman law in the middle
ages is said to have been derived. These southern
republics disappeared for ever. Their sisters of the North
were more fortunate in their destiny. Venice, founded by
fugitives who sought refuge among the lagoons of the
Adriatic from the invasion of Attila and his Huns,
established its capital on the Rialto in 809. Its be-
ginnings were humble and obscure. We shall find that
at the close of the middle ages, after a career of
irregular prosperity and glory, it still holds rank among
the chief powers of Europe. The republics of Pisa and
Genoa came earlier to maturity, and suffered an earlier
fate. They wore out their strength in perpetual and
barren rivalry. Pisa still attests, by its marble cathedral,
its leaning bell tower, and its burial ground, furnished with
the holy earth of Gethsemane, and glowing with the frescoes
of Orcagna, the place which it once held amongst the

cities of the Mediterranean. But the port is silted up, grass grows in the streets, and the walls enclose a space far too large for its inhabitants. It first fell before the maritime rivalry of Genoa, and then became part of the land empire of Florence. Genoa still flourishes as part of an united Italy, and extends its commerce at the cost of Marseilles. But it spent in selfish money-making the strength which Venice used in the creation of an Eastern empire, and in resistance to the advancing Turk.

The beginning of the twelfth century witnessed the rise of Milan to a position of supremacy over the towns in the valley of the Po. Under the later Roman Empire this town had been the rival of Rome. As the see of St Ambrose and at a later period of St Carlo Borromeo it twice took the lead in ecclesiastical reform ; sometimes the asserter of liberty, sometimes the home of despotism, at one time enslaved and destroyed, at another wealthy and triumphant —it represented in its own vicissitudes the varying fortunes of the Lombard plain.

The death of Henry V. in 1125 gave prominence to two factions whose names are intimately associated with the internal wars of Italy. The Salian or Franconian Emperors, the descendants of Conrad, were also known by the name of Waiblingen from a castle which they occupied in the diocese of Augsburg. The house of Bavaria having had many princes of the name of Wölf, came to be generally known by this appellation. The two words were Italianized into Ghibellino and Guelfo, and as the later Salic emperors had been enemies of the church, the two parties ranged themselves respectively on the sides of the empire and the papacy. Also, as a general rule, the Ghibellines supported the principles of strong governance, and the Guelphs those of freedom and self-rule. These differences did not break out into open flame until the expedition of Frederick Barbarossa into Italy. Elected Emperor in 1152, he passed into Italy in 1154. He came there on the invitation of the Pope, of the Prince of Capua, and of the towns which had been subjected to the ambition of Milan. He marched at the head of his German feudatories, a splendid and imposing array. His first object was to crush the power of Milan, and to exalt that of Pavia, the head of a rival league. Nothing could stand against him. At Viterbo he was compelled to hold the stirrup of the Pope, and in return for this submission he received the crown from the Pontiff's hands in the Basilica of St Peter. He returned northwards by the valley of the Tiber, dismissed his army at Ancona, and with difficulty escaped safely into Bavaria. His passage left little that was solid and durable behind it. He had effected nothing against the King of Naples. His friendship with the Pope was illusory and short-lived. The dissensions of the North which had been hushed for a moment by his presence, broke out again as soon as his back was turned. He had, however, received the crown of Charles the Great from the hands of the successor of St Peter. But Frederick was not a man to brook easily the miscarriage of his designs. In 1158 he collected another army at Ulm. Brescia was quickly subdued ; Lodi, which had been destroyed by the Milanese, was rebuilt, and Milan itself was reduced to terms. This peace lasted but for a short time ; Milan revolted, and was placed under the ban of the Empire. The fate of Cremona taught the Milanese what they had to expect from the clemency of the Emperor. After a desultory warfare, regular siege was laid to the town. On March 1, 1162, Milan, reduced by famine, surrendered at discretion, and a fortnight later all the inhabitants were ordered to leave the town. The circuit of the walls was partitioned out among the most pitiless enemies of its former greatness, and the inhabitants of Lodi, of Cremona, of Pavia, of Novara, and of Como were encouraged to wreak their vengeance on their defeated rival. For six days the imperial army laboured to overturn the walls and public buildings, and when the Emperor left for Pavia on Palm Sunday 1162, not a fiftieth part of the city was standing. This terrible vengeance produced a violent reaction. The homeless fugitives were received by their ancient enemies, and local jealousies were merged in common hatred of the common foe. Frederick had already been excommunicated by Pope Alexander III. as the supporter of his rival Victor. Verona undertook to be the public vindicator of discontent. Five years after the destruction of Milan the Lombard league numbered fifteen towns amongst its members. Venice, Verona, Vicenza, Treviso, Ferrara, Brescia, Bergamo, Cremona, Milan, Lodi, Piacenza, Parma, Modena, and Bologna. The confederation solemnly engaged to expel the Emperor from Italy. The towns on the frontier of Piedmont asked and obtained admission to the league, and to mark the dawn of freedom a new town was founded on the low marshy ground which is drained by the Bormida and the Tanaro, and which afterwards witnessed the victory of Marengo. It was named by its founders Alessandria, in honour of the Pope, who had vindicated their independence of the Empire. It was named by the Ghibellines, in derision of its filthy squalor, Alessandria della Paglia, Alessandria, the town of straw. The Lombard league had unfortunately a very imperfect constitution. It had no common treasure, no uniform rules for the apportionment of contributions; it existed solely for the purposes of defence against the external foe. The time was not yet come when self-sacrifice and self-abnegation could lay the foundations of a united Italy. Frederick spent six years in preparing vengeance. In 1174 he laid siege to the new Alexandria, but did not succeed in taking it. A severe struggle took place two years later. In 1176 a new army arrived from Germany, and on May 29 Frederick Barbarossa was entirely defeated at Legnano. In 1876 the seventh hundred anniversary of the battle was celebrated on the spot where it was gained, and it is still regarded as the birthday of Italian freedom. The last years of Frederick do not concern us. In his old age he assumed the badge of a Crusader, and was drowned in 1190 in the river Kalikadnos in Armenia.

Two great personalities now claim our attention on the scene of history — Pope Innocent III. and the Emperor Frederick II. Their career fills up the period between the death of Frederick Barbarossa and the date chosen for the commencement of our detailed history. Innocent III. was elected Pope in the year 1199, at the age of thirty-seven. He completed the fabric of the papal power, the foundations of which had been laid by Hildebrand. The dissensions of the Empire gave opportunity for the assertion of the Pope's authority. Frederick II., infant son of the last emperor, Henry VI., was left as the ward of Innocent, having been created King of the Romans during his father's lifetime. His succession to the Imperial crown was disputed by Philip, Duke of Swabia, and by Otho of the Bavarian and Saxon line. Innocent warmly supported the cause of his ward, with the object of increasing and extending the power of the tiara. He placed the city of Rome under the government of a senator, who was able to curb the excesses of the turbulent nobles. He established three Guelphic leagues against the power of the emperor—one in the *march* or seaboard of the Adriatic, another in the valley of the Tiber, and the third in Tuscany. He held the language of imperious command to every court in Europe. He ordered Andrew, King of Hungary, to undertake a crusade ; the kings of Denmark and Sweden to depose the King of Norway ; Philip Augustus of France to take back the wife whom he had repudiated. He forced the proudest sovereigns to receive their crowns from his hands—the King of Portugal, the King of Arragon, the King of Poland, and the King of England. At last he found himself face to face with Otho IV., Emperor of Germany. Otho received the imperial crown from the Pope's hands, and there was a transient gleam of peace and amity. But their short-lived friendship was soon broken, by the strain of divergent interests. Open war broke out between Otho and Frederick. Innocent succeeded in all his enterprises, the power of Otho was broken at the battle of Bouvines in 1214, a victory which gave the first impulse to the aggrandisement of France at the expense of Germany. Frederick was amused and deluded by the hope of the Imperial crown. In his last years the Pope had leisure to turn his arms against the Manichæan heretics, who, starting from the mountains of Bulgaria, carried their pure but stern religion westwards in a constant stream which never lost touch with its fountain-head, and under the names of Paterini, Ketzer, and Albigenses earned the execration of their contemporaries, and the respect of posterity. Innocent died in 1211, and Otho lived only two years longer.

Frederick II. is one of the most picturesque and fascinating characters in history. King of Sicily at four years old, he grew up to manhood under the protection of the Pope. He was one of the most cultivated men of a cultivated age. He spoke Latin, French, German, Greek, and Arabic; he was one of the first to give importance to the Italian tongue. His court was crowded with literary men, he was himself an author of repute. He was the paragon of knightly virtues and accomplishments, free and secular in his opinions and habits. The great valley of central Italy, which is shut off by two parallel chains of Apennines, from the Mediterranean and Adriatic Sea, is full of his towers, his churches, and his castles. When he received the imperial crown from Pope Honorius III. in 1220, there seemed a fair hope that the quarrel between Church and State might be for ever appeased, and that they might reign with similar but unequal power, like the sun and moon in heaven. But the thirty years which followed were full of misery and disaster. Frederick was excommunicated because he did not go to the Crusade; he was excommunicated because he went. Gregory succeeded Honorius, and Innocent, Gregory. At each vacancy of the Holy See Frederick sued for peace. Saint Louis of France interceded for a king who had saved an army of Crusaders at Cyprus, but each succeeding pope excommunicated and deposed the emperor, and absolved his subjects from their allegiance. Three forces were especially arrayed against him; the principal of which was that of the popes as heads of the Guelphic party. The rival interests of Guelphs and Ghibellines were too real to slumber or to be concealed. The success of a Ghibelline emperor meant the subjection of Italy to Germany, the binding of north and south together in an unnatural union, the establishment of a great power in Europe fatal to the freedom of the nations. Innocent III. had made use of Frederick whilst he was too weak to repel a more formidable foe. His successors broke with this hollow and impossible alliance. Frederick was also opposed by the resistance of the Lombard league. He was, it is true, very different to Barbarossa. He was an Italian to the backbone, and had he been accepted as sovereign, his power in Germany might have slipped away from him. But he was emperor, and a Hohenstauffen, and the towns of Italy loved liberty with the danger of anarchy, rather than unity with the possibility of subjection. In the third place, he was at variance with the spiritual powers which were at work in Italy during this period. Innocent III. had established the two great orders of Franciscans and Dominicans as a support to the papacy. It is difficult to exaggerate the influence which these friars have had on the development of the Italian people. But there is a striking contrast between the poverty, chastity, and obedience of the Franciscan brotherhood, and the gay, light-hearted, dissolute, and free-thinking court of the brilliant emperor. Never were the church and the world brought into sharper antagonism. Frederick died at Ferentino on December 13, 1250. With his death a new era begins for Italy, one in which purely Italian forces reach their highest activity and development. This period will form the subject of the present work.

CHAPTER II.

GUELPHS AND GHIBELLINES—EZZELINO DA ROMANO— EARLY VENICE.

AFTER the death of Frederick II., an interval of twenty-three years passed without the appointment of a king of the Romans (1250-1273), and an interval of sixty years without the recognition of an emperor in Italy (1250-1309). The country therefore was left to govern itself, but it was not at all the less divided by discords and distracted by dissensions. The parties of Guelph and Ghibelline raged as fiercely as if the lances of the German hosts were ever glimmering on the crest of the Alps, or as if the Lombard leagues were in constant watchfulness against an impending foe. These two party names occur again and again in history, until the time when both factions were crushed beneath the heel of a common enemy. They represented divergent principles, although in the heat of conflict all question of principle was too often disregarded. The origin of these two parties has been already mentioned. We will now attempt to define the ideas which they embodied. Speaking generally, the Ghibellines were the party of the emperor, and the Guelphs the party of the Pope; the Ghibellines were on the side of authority, or sometimes of oppression, the Guelphs were on the side of liberty and self-government. Again, the Ghibellines were the supporters of an universal empire of which Italy was to be the head, the Guelphs were on the side of national life and national

individuality.   The refrain of the Garibaldian war-song,
which bids the stranger to leave the plains of Italy, might
have been the battle-cry of the Guelph.   If these definitions
could be considered as exhaustive, there would be little doubt
as to the side to which our sympathies should be given.
Frederick II., although he was in early life supported by a
Pope, was yet in heart a Ghibelline.   The later measures of
his government, especially after the year 1232, were directed
to the entire destruction of the feudal state and the
reduction of his subjects to the condition of a multitude
destitute of will, but profitable to the exchequer.   He was
penetrated with Saracenic views of organisation; he cared
little for liberty or for constitutional government.   On the
other hand, Thomas Aquinas, the great philosopher of
the Roman church, sketched out a perfect constitution, in
which the prince was supported by an upper house, while a
lower house of representatives was chosen by the people,
and they were secured against oppression by the right of
revolution.   We should thus expect all patriots to be
Guelphs, and the Ghibelline party to be composed of men
who were too spiritless to resist despotic power, or too
selfish to surrender it.   But, on the other hand, we must
never forget that Dante was a Ghibelline.   No man ever
yearned more passionately for the advent of a saviour from
beyond the Alps; no man ever more persistently endeavoured to restrain the papacy within the limits of its
spiritual power.   Therefore we see that the question is not
a simple one.   The party of the Guelphs was subject to
many weaknesses.   It had an ecclesiastic at its head; the
national party was exposed to all the stormy dissensions
and complicated intrigues which afflicted the papal court.
First amongst the causes of these troubles was the un-

natural confusion between religious and civil sanctions. Under the papal government every crime was a sin, every offender against the State was liable to be punished by excommunication. Again, the Pope, although he represented the unity of Italy, did not scruple to call in the assistance of the foreigner. Three times did three several Charles's of the house of France cross the Alps and devastate the plains of Italy to fight the battles of the Pontiff. The Church was more anxious for the accomplishment of its private ends than for the liberation of Italian territory. Macchiavelli represents the views of the best political thinkers of his age when he argues that the truest hope of regeneration for Italy lies in the exclusion of the clergy from civil offices. It was a constant weakness to the Guelph party that it had the Pope as its leader. But in the course of a minute and fretful struggle the objects of both parties had been confused and half forgotten. They had become mere party cries, mixed with a hundred associations of ancestral hatreds and inherited feuds. In some cities the parties had received new names, in others one or other of them had split up into sections as divergent and as bitter as the dissensions of the parent stocks. In the fourteenth century there was scarcely a city in Italy which was not distracted by the bloodthirsty quarrels of a traditional vendetta. It might well be urged, Who should still this raging sea, but the commanding voice of Cæsar? what force should weld these chaotic elements into a living organism, except the strong hand of imperial power? This was the view of Dante. He who had seen nothing but order and harmony in the spheres of Paradise, preferred even tyranny to the confusion which reminded him of the turmoils of the circles of hell. The history of Florence at this time offers a good example of the struggles of the two parties. The city, although its sympathies were mainly Guelph, was divided into two sections. Frederick had driven out the Guelph and established the Ghibelline in its place. Immediately after his death the Guelph exiles were recalled. This was a time, as the historian Villani tells us, of great simplicity of manners, a simplicity which Dante is constantly regretting. On October 20, 1250, even before the death of the Emperor, the people rose in rebellion against the power of the nobles. They met in the square before the church of Santa Croce, the Westminster Abbey of Florence, the burial-place of its illustrious dead, deposed the podestà, established a Government consisting of a *signoria* of twelve members, two chosen from each of the six wards of the town, renewable every two months. They then formed a national militia to defend their independence ; they pulled down the fortresses of the nobles, and built out of the materials a public palace for their magistrates, the present *bargello*, the chapel in which contains what is believed to be the portrait of Dante painted by Giotto. After the return of the Guelph exiles, steps were taken to gain over the neighbouring cities to the Guelph cause. Lucca was the only town which had given its adherence to that party. Pistoia, Siena, Pisa, Volterra, were Ghibelline. The success of this movement was extremely rapid. Pistoia soon submitted, the Pisans were driven within their walls, and the territory of Siena was overrun. In memory of these events, the Florentines coined for the first time their gold florin stamped with the emblem of the *giglio* or lily. Though changed in weight and fineness the florin existed until within the memory of men now living. The year 1254, which the Florentines called the year of victories, witnessed the final triumph over Siena, Pisa, and Volterra.

Ten years later the epoch of vengeance arrived. In 1258 the Ghibelline nobles, who had lived peaceably under the popular government, were driven out because they were suspected of conspiracy. They had recourse to Manfred, king of Sicily, the natural son of Frederick II., who had assumed the crown as the representative of his nephew Conradin. The Ghibelline exiles, the chief of whom was Farinata degli Uberti, had taken refuge in Siena, a city always true to the Ghibelline cause. Florence declared war against the town; Manfred sent a small company of a hundred men to its assistance. By the machinations of Farinata, this puny force was cut to pieces, and the banner of the king of Sicily was trailed in the dust. The honour of Manfred was engaged, and he dispatched a large contingent to avenge the insult. Farinata again displayed his adroitness by stirring up the Florentines to a premature attack. On October 4, 1260, was fought the battle of Montaperti, sometimes called the battle of the Arbia, the first great shock of arms between Guelphs and Ghibellines. On the Florentine side were collected soldiers from all the Guelph cities, Pistoia, Prato, San Miniato, San Gemignano, and Colle di Val d'Elsa. This party was superior in numbers to their enemies, but they were surprised and surrounded by the Germans of Manfred and the Ghibelline exiles whom they had expelled. The hand which bore the standard of Florence was cleft in two by the sword of a traitor: the Guelph army was utterly defeated. Florence alone lost two thousand five hundred men; there was scarcely a family which had not to lament the loss of one of its members. Of the Guelph army ten thousand were killed, and many more were taken prisoners. The condition of Florence after this defeat was terrible indeed. It was sunk in hopeless apathy and despair. The citizens were equally afraid of treachery from within and vengeance from without. Nine days after the battle the chiefs of the Guelph party left the city with their wives and children, and were scattered amongst the neighbouring cities. Similar scenes took place within the walls of their allied towns. Lucca still remained unconquered, and received the fragments of the defeated party. The Ghibelline exiles re-entered Florence, and the city took the oath of allegiance to Manfred.

In the meantime a diet of representatives from Ghibelline cities came together at Empoli, and deliberated on the best means of consolidating their interests. The envoys of Pisa and Venice urged that there was only one way of securing a lasting peace, to destroy the city which had made itself the nursing mother of the Guelphs, and to raze Florence to the ground. Then Farinata degli Uberti, to whom the victory was due, rose proud and disdainful, as Dante saw him afterwards in the pit of hell, and cried, "Know that if I remained alone amongst all the men of Florence I would not suffer my country to be destroyed, and that if it were necessary to die a thousand deaths for her, a thousand deaths would I willingly die." He then left the assembly. The Ghibellines rejected the base proposal of their allies, and confined themselves to establishing in Florence a militia of a thousand men under the command of Guido Novello, whom they had made *podestà* of Florence.

Whilst the towns of Tuscany were thus falling under the power of the Ghibellines, the northern plains of Lombardy and of the valley of the Po were forgetting the noble traditions of the Lombard League. The most prominent figure in this part of Italy at this time was Ezzelino da Romano, lord of Padua. In 1250 he was fifty-six years of age, and had reigned for twenty-five years. He had married the daughter of Frederick II. The world has probably never seen so barbarous a monster. He had no regular system of government or administration, but attempted to found an empire by wholesale murder. One of the first acts of the new Pope, Alexander IV., in 1255, was to proclaim a crusade against him, and to call upon all good Christians to hunt him down like a wild beast. The cause was indeed a worthy one. After the death of Frederick, Ezzelino had thrown aside what shreds of decency that hitherto veiled his actions. Padua had become a charnel house. When his victims had died in his prisons, Ezzelino sent their corpses to their native towns to be beheaded in the market place. Nobles were slain by his satellites in crowds, their bodies cut in pieces and burnt. The whole town resounded with the groans of the tortured and the dying. Every kind of excellence fell a victim to his fury. Birth, wealth, learning, piety, beauty and promise were held to be sufficient cause to justify a disgraceful death.

The war against Ezzelino began in 1256. Venice placed herself at the head of the crusade. Ezzelino had made himself master of Verona, Vicenza, Padua, Feltre, and Belluno. Padua was captured by a *coup-de-main*. Ezzelino repaid himself for this insult by a terrible revenge. A third of his army consisted of soldiers levied either in Padua itself or in the surrounding districts. By a cruel stratagem he persuaded these men to surrender themselves, threw them into prison, and put them all to death. The war continued for several years. Ezzelino depended on the assistance of the Lombard nobles, but they were gradually estranged by his cruelty and faithlessness. After taking the castle of

Priola, situated between Bassano and Vicenza, he condemned all the inhabitants—men, women, and children, lay and cleric—to the same punishment. He put out their eyes, cut off their noses and their legs, and sent them to crawl mutilated about the country and beg for alms. At length, in 1259, Ezzelino was taken prisoner at Cassano, after being wounded, and died by his own hands. All the towns which had been subjected to his tyranny submitted to the Pope and to the Guelphic league.

Although this danger had been got rid of, no town in the northern plains of Italy, except Venice, was able to establish a durable republic. The poet tells us that liberty has two voices, one of the sea, and the other of the mountains. Freedom dwells upon the heights, and not upon the plains. The plains of Lombardy were peculiarly suited to the evolutions of cavalry, and cavalry was especially the arm of the nobles, as infantry was of the citizens in the towns. Hence the great towns Milan, Verona, and Padua, were no sooner free from one master than they fell under the dominion of another. This encroachment was also assisted by the fact that the towns were obliged to allow themselves to be defended by some nobles of their choice against the attack of a robber chieftain who might swoop down upon them from the mountains. They were obliged to oppose cavalry of their own to the cavalry of their enemies. We find the power of more than one of these houses raised upon the ruins of the authority of Ezzelino. The house of Della Torre was established at Milan, to be succeeded in its turn by the houses of Visconti and Sforza. Verona now committed itself to the family of Della Scala, who reigned with unsullied glory for more than two centuries, who offered an asylum to the exiled Dante, and gave a Scaliger to scholarship. Ferrara entrusted itself to the house of Este, that illustrious line, linked with the fortunes of the poet Tasso, and through Brunswick with the throne of England. On the whole the Guelph party gained but little by the overthrow of Ezzelino. The Pope found himself encompassed by Ghibellines on the south, and on the north, and our succeeding narrative will show what steps he took to recover his power, and to rescue himself from his enemies.

It will now be convenient to give a sketch of the early history of Venice, which had an existence apart from the other towns of Northern Italy. It knew of no struggles between Ghibellines and Guelphs, as its attention was mainly directed to the commerce of the East. Founded as an off-shoot from Aquileia amongst the islands and lagoons at the head of the Adriatic Gulf, it was at first governed as a part of the Eastern Empire. The power of the exarchate of Ravenna now became too weak to control it, and the isolated community elected rulers or Doges of its own. At first these elections showed a strong tendency to be continued in the same family, and precautions were taken to prevent the office from becoming hereditary. In 1032 two counsellors were placed at the side of the Doge, whose consent should be necessary to any determination which he might take. Their number was afterwards increased to six, one for each ward of the city, and there were added to the government the three heads of the *quarantia*, or great court of justice. The Doge was from the first elected for life. This body of ten formed the chief executive and administrative power of the Republic. The great council, the *gran consiglio*, representing the people, consisted in its earliest form of 480 members. It was chosen by a method of double election. The people chose two electors from

each *sestiere* or ward.   Each of these twelve chose forty
councillors from his own part of the city.   Not more than
four members might be taken from the same family.   It
has been already stated that the administration of justice
was committed to a *quarantia* or council of forty, established
for the first time in 1179.   Besides the said cabinet of
twelve, and the popular body nearly as large as our House
of Commons, there was an intermediate senate or council
of *pregadi*.   There, as their name implies, had been at first
persons *prayed* or invited by the Doge to assist him with
their counsel and advice.   In 1229 they became a regular
part of the constitution.   Their number was then fixed at
sixty, and they were nominated by the great council; their
business was to prepare measures for the great council, and
to watch over commercial and foreign affairs.   Such were
the features of the ordinary constitution; on grave and
important occasions an appeal was made to the people as a
whole.   The popular assembly was called Arrengo at
Venice and Parliamento at Florence.   By gradual steps the
power of the Arrengo was abolished, that of the Gran
Consiglio confirmed, and that of the Doge limited in every
direction, until the State was eventually governed by a close
oligarchy of prosperous merchants.   We may anticipate
chronologers by completing this sketch of the development
of the Venetian constitution.   In 1229 two new sets of
officers were appointed, the Cinque correttori della pro-
mission ducale, whose duty it was to revise the oath taken
by the Doge at his election, and the three Inquisitori del
Doge defunto whose business was to enquire into the conduct of the late Doge, and, if necessary, to condemn his
memory and to fine his heirs.   The duty of laying these
matters before the high court was committed to public

prosecutors, the *avogadori* of the republic. The promise of
the Doge was a species of national charter which might be
amended at each avoidance of the office. In 1172 the
election of the Doge had been transferred from the people
to Gran Consiglio. The council delegated for this purpose,
first twenty-four and then forty members, reduced by lot to
eleven. In the middle of the thirteenth century the
method of the election of the Doge became more complicated. The members of the grand council who were over
thirty years of age drew from a bag balls partly gilt and
partly silvered. The thirty who drew the gilded balls again
cast lots for nine of their number, whose business it was to
appoint forty men of different families, seven out of the nine
voices being necessary for a choice. These forty drew
lots for twelve of their number; the twelve chose twenty-
five, each of whom required to have nine votes for his
election. The five-and-twenty cast lots for nine, the nine
chose forty-five, each of whom needed seven voices for his
election. This body of five-and-forty, after taking an oath
to make a choice according to their conscience, threw the
names of the persons whom they wished to appoint Doge
into a vessel. If the votes were found to be scattering,
they repeated the process until twenty-five were given for
one person, who was then declared elected. Such was the
jealous nature of this close oligarchy.

The Venetians took but a moderate interest in the
affairs of Italy. In the twelfth century Dandolo had established himself at Constantinople, and in 1225 it was
debated whether the capital of the Republic should not be
transferred to the shores of the Bosphorus. This was not
carried, but many islands of the Ægean sea were partitioned
as fiefs amongst noble families; and Crete especially was

formed into an image of the mother state, with a Doge of
its own and a hierarchy of privileged nobles.   In 1661,
when Crete was captured by the Turks, the Candian nobles
were transferred to the *Libro d'oro*, the Golden Book, the
register of the Venetian nobility.   A war broke out between
Venice and Genoa, which had the effect of detaching
Venice from the Guelf cause, and allying her with the
Ghibelline Pisa.   This new alliance was an additional reason
why the Pope should strain every nerve to preserve his party,
and should employ the somewhat questionable methods
which will be treated of in the ensuing chapter.

CHAPTER III.

CHARLES OF ANJOU—MANFRED—CONRADIN—
SICILIAN VESPERS.

WHILST the Ghibelline party was pushing its advance
in the north of Italy, it was not less successful in the
south.   Here its cause was maintained by Manfred,
king of Sicily, the natural son of Frederick II.   In 1261
Pope Alexander IV. died, and was succeeded by Urban
IV., a Frenchman of humble birth.   Immediately after
his election he directed his efforts to the revival of
the Guelphic party.   He turned against Manfred with
savage zeal.   He attempted, but in vain, to prevent the
marriage of Constance, the daughter of Manfred, with the
son of James, King of Arragon, an alliance which gave
the house of Arragon a claim to the throne of Sicily.   In
his weakness and despair he naturally turned for assistance
to Louis IX., king of France.   It was natural that, as a
Frenchman, he should seek help from his own sovereign,
and that, as Pope, he should approach with confidence the
most pious monarch in Christendom.   The Pope offered the
crown of Naples to Charles of Anjou, brother of St Louis.
Charles was at this time forty-five years of age.   He held
the country of Anjou as a fief of the crown of France, and
the country of Provence, which he held in right of his wife,
placed him almost on an equality with the reigning sovereigns
of Europe.   His stern and cold but energetic character

stands out in strange contrast to that of Charles VIII., who
followed him in a similar expedition two hundred years
afterwards.   Just as Charles of Anjou was on the point
of marching into Italy, and Manfred was marshalling
his Saracens to oppose him, Urban IV. died.   The
sacred college, however, consisted mainly of cardinals of
his nomination, and they chose as his successor Clement
IV., who was, if possible, more closely devoted than Urban
to the interests of the French.   He invested the army of
Charles with the character of crusaders, and treated the
war against Manfred as a sacred war.   Charles took
the command of a fleet.   He escaped the cruisers of
Manfred, and, with a thousand chosen soldiers sailed
up the Tiber to Rome.   In the meantime his wife led
an army of thirty thousand men across the passes of
the Alps.   As the Pope was at Perugia Charles was
crowned king of the two Sicilies by commission.   He
accepted the following conditions.   First, that in the case
of failure of heirs the crown should revert to the Church;
secondly, that it should be tenable with the diadem of the
empire as the lordship of Lombardy or Tuscany; and
thirdly, that he would cede to the Pope the duchy of
Beneventum and pay a subsidy to the Roman See.   The
two armies of Manfred and Charles met in the plain of
Beneventum, not far from the place where the power of
Rome was for a time destroyed by Hannibal in the battle of
Cannæ.   Manfred desired to negotiate, but Charles replied
to him, " Go and tell the Sultan of Nocera that I wish for
nothing but a battle, and that to-day I will either send him
to hell or he shall send me to Paradise."   Manfred was
utterly defeated, and lost his life and his crown.   His naked
body was brought to Charles thrown across a donkey's back,

and was denied Christian burial. It was first thrown into a pit at the end of the bridge of Beneventum, and each soldier of the army as he passed by cast a stone upon the body. At a later period the bones of the heretic monarch were cast out of the kingdom by the order of the Archbishop of Cosenza, and exposed upon the banks of the Rio Verde. The battle was fought on Friday, February 26, 1266. Manfred's wife and children were thrown into prison, and afterwards put to death; the city of Beneventum was ravaged and destroyed.

The victory of Charles had the effect of reviving the Guelph party at Florence. Guido Novello, Count of Batifolle, who since the battle of Montaperti had been the head of the Ghibelline party in that city, saw the necessity of coming to terms with his adversaries. Twelve guilds or corporations were formed, seven of them of the higher occupations, the *arti maggiori*, such as the jurisconsults, the bankers, the *calimala*, or the makers of fine Italian cloth, and five of the *arti minori*, the tanners, butchers, and cobblers. Then was formed the nucleus of a commercial aristocracy which was to play an important part in the future history of the city. But in the spring of 1269 Charles established the Guelph party in power with the help of eight hundred cavalry under the command of Guy of Montfort, son of the famous Earl of Leicester, the Father of the English Parliament.

Charles was not allowed to hold the crown of the two Sicilies without a struggle. A young lad was preparing in the heart of Germany an expedition to recover the possessions of his father. The legitimate son of Frederick II. was the Emperor Conrad IV. Conrad had, at his death, left a young son, also named Conrad, but better known as Con-

radin.   Manfred did not deny his claim, and affected to
hold the kingdom of Naples in his name.   Conradin was
now at the threshold of early manhood.   He had just been
married, and had been educated by his mother, Elizabeth,
at the court of Bavaria, in full knowledge of the rights
to which he was heir.   He had always refused to fight
against Manfred for the recovery of his interests, but
he was now assailed by the entreaties of the different
sections of the Ghibelline party that he would set himself to attack the usurper Charles.   The old comrades
of Manfred urged the youth to avenge his father.   The
Ghibellines of Tuscany promised their assistance.   The
great nobles of the valley of the Po assured him
that they were holding their armies at his disposi-
tion.   The French were represented as outraging every
right of God and man ; Conradin, it was said, would
be received as a deliverer by the population of Italy.   He
could not resist the urgency of these offers, supported by
the instincts of his own chivalrous nature, and the keen
remembrance of his private wrong.   His cousin, Frederick
of Austria, only a few years older than himself, whose
estates were at this time occupied by Ottocar, king of
Bohemia, offered to share his danger.   After taking an
affecting leave of his mother and wife at Hohenschwangau,
that romantic nest of lakes in which the ill-fated Ludwig
of Bavaria found a congenial home, Conrad crossed the
Brenner, and arrived at Verona towards the end of the year
1267, with an army of three thousand five hundred men.
He traversed Lombardy without difficulty, and was soon
encouraged by two unexpected advantages.   Rome and
Sicily declared for his cause.   The post of Senator of
Rome was, at this time, held by Henry of Castile, cousin

of Charles of Anjou, and Frederick of Castile, his brother, had roused Sicily to support the Swabian cause. At the same time the Saracen soldiers of Manfred raised the standard of revolt in Apulia.

Conradin was received with enthusiasm by the Ghibelline cities of Pisa and Siena. On Easter day 1268, the Pope, who was then at Viterbo, who had repeatedly summoned the lad to lay down his arms, solemnly excommunicated him. The young prince, by way of reply, paraded his army before the walls of the city. Clement, as he saw Conradin and Frederick of Austria ride past him at the head of their troops, exclaimed to his cardinals—" Behold the victims who are being led to the sacrifice." Conradin left Rome, where he had been well received, on August 18, to march into the kingdom of Naples. The most natural road for him to take would have led through the great Latin plain, which, stretching far to the south behind the Alban Mount unites itself with the rich expanse of Campania Felix. But the banks of the Garigliano and the fortresses which defend the kingdom on this side were well manned, and Conradin's army was not large. He determined, therefore, to turn aside to Tivoli, and by rough mountain roads to reach that central heart of Italy where his grandfather had reigned supreme, and which he had covered with castles and cities of a unique and beautiful architecture.

After his passage across the hills Conradin reached the town of Tagliacozzo, and descended by its steep streets into the plain which was at that time enclosed at its further end by the waters of the Fucine lakes. Of him it might be said, as of the priest Umbo, " Te nemus Anguitiae, vitrea te Fucinus unda, te liquidi flevere lacus." [1] The plain is of large extent, on

_____
[1] Æneid vii. 759.

its eastern side rise low and gently sloping hills, crowned by the old Roman garrison town of Alba Fucentia, whose massive walls are still nearly entire, and by the mediæval town of Scurgola. At a little distance lies the castle and city of Celano—the castle, one of the finest works of Frederick II. ; the town, the birthplace of Thomas of Celano, the author of that noble requiem hymn the *Dies iræ*. Charles had reached the plain by crossing the steep mountain range over which runs the road from Aquila. Such was the field on which was to be fought what is perhaps the most important battle of the middle ages, known to us by the name of Tagliacozzo, but it might more fitly bear the name of Scurgola. The numbers were unequal. Conradin had five thousand horsemen, Charles had only three thousand, and the issue of the battle might have been different, had not a stratagem been suggested to Charles by an old French knight, Alard de St Valéry, who had just arrived on his way from the Holy Land, like Desaix at the battle of Marengo. By his advice Charles divided his army into three portions, two of which he set to guard the bridge over the river which traverses the plain. For the third he chose the flower of his host, and placing himself at their head hid them in a small valley where they could not be seen by Conradin. The charge of the Germans was impetuous, the French army was entirely put to rout; Henry of Cosenza was killed; St Valéry could scarcely restrain the impatience of the king. At length the fitting moment arrived. The German troops were scattered over the plain in small bodies reaping the fruits of their victory. Then the horsemen placed in ambush were let loose upon them and the army of Conradin was entirely defeated. Henry of Castile appeared in the field with his Spanish troops too late to give assistance, and was soon made prisoner. Conradin and Frederick galloped from the scene of disaster, and did not draw rein until they reached the sea. As they were attempting to escape to Sicily, they were captured by one of the Frangipani, and imprisoned in the castle of Astura. Their end may be told in a few words. Frangipani was forced to give up his prisoners, and they were confined at Naples. Charles went through the mockery of trying Conradin as a rebel against himself, his legitimate sovereign. The arguments of justice were on one side, those of force on the other. The sentence of death was announced to Conradin as he sat playing chess with his cousin Frederick. He was executed in the public square of Naples. Just before his death he exclaimed, "How will my mother grieve when she hears of this," and threw his glove into the midst of the crowd, to be taken up by anyone who would avenge his death. Frederick of Austria and Conradin's chief supporters met with the same fate; Henry of Castile was spared. Conradin was the last of the line of Hohenstauffen, and his was the last serious attempt to establish the authority of Germany over the whole of Italy, and to make the peninsula dependent on the imperial crown. It was strange that the deliverance of Italy should have been effected by a French army, against the wishes of the Italian people. We have seen in our own age the first impulse to Italian unity, and to the expulsion of the Austrians from the country given by a French army at the battle of Solferino. On the other hand, it has been remarked that the death of Conradin at Naples was avenged by the surrender of Napoleon III. at Sedan. The battle of Tagliacozzo took place on August 23; the death of Conradin on October 29, 1268.

Charles reigned for seventeen years after the defeat of
Conradin, and died in January 1285. The most important
event during this portion of his reign was the massacre of
the French in Sicily, commonly called the Sicilian Vespers.
In order to understand this event we must remember, first,
that there was a claimant to the throne of Sicily in the
person of Peter of Arragon, son of James, who had married
Constance, the daughter of Manfred; and, generally, that
the position of Charles depended upon the character and
sympathies of the Pope for the time being, and that these
were liable to constant change. Pope Clement IV. died
just one month after the execution of Conradin, after
which there was a vacancy of the Holy See for thirty-three
months. This was favourable to the growth of Charles's
power, and during this period he took part in the crusade
of his brother Saint Louis. In 1271, an Italian, Tebaldo,
Viscount of Piacenza, was elected Pope, taking the name
of Gregory X. The chief object of his life was the recovery
of the Holy Land from the infidels, and for this purpose he
did his best to reconcile the two parties of Guelph and
Ghibelline. He succeeded in making peace between the
two factions at Florence; he appeased the differences between the Genoese and Charles of Anjou; he put an end
to the war which had broken out between Venice and
Bologna. But he saw that one of the most fruitful causes
of disunion and anarchy was the interregnum of the imperial crown, and he did not hesitate to secure the election
of a strong emperor and to establish a formidable rival to the
papal power. After the death of Frederick II. the imperial
throne remained vacant or disputed for many years.
Conrad IV. was recognised as king of Germany by the
Ghibellines, and William of Holland by the Guelphs. In

1257, Richard, Earl of Cornwall, and Alphonso, king of Castile, had been elected kings of the Romans by rival factions. Richard died in 1271. Alphonso still desired to preserve his title, but it was not recognised by the Pope. At length, in 1273, the German electors, yielding to the entreaties of the Supreme Pontiff, elected Rudolph of Hapsburgh emperor. He was received by the German princes, by the Pope, and by the Church, although he was never crowned at Rome. He was the founder of a long line of emperors, who gradually converted an elective into an hereditary monarchy, and his descendants sit on the throne of Austria at the present day. The last exploit of Gregory X. was to receive the submission of the Greek emperor, Michael Palæologus, and to draw up at the Council of Lyons rules which were to secure the speedy election of future Popes. They are in force at the present time, and are a safeguard against the occurrence of an interregnum such as that which preceded his own election. Gregory was preparing to terminate his reign by a great crusade against the infidels in the Holy Land, in which the kings of France, England, Arragon, and Sicily should take part, under the command of the Emperor in person, but before this could be accomplished he died suddenly in January 1276. It will be seen that the pontificate of Gregory X., however conducive to the peace of Europe, was not calculated to develop the power of Charles of Anjou.

After the death of Gregory three popes succeeded each other in rapid succession in the space of a single year, Innocent V., Adrian V., and John XX. In 1277 Nicholas III., of the House of Orsini, was raised to the tiara, and reigned for three years. He showed plainly that he intended to follow in the footsteps of Gregory X. He persuaded Charles to resign his protectorate over Tuscany, and attempted to confine him within the limits of the two Sicilies. By encouraging the Emperor Rudolf to expect a solemn coronation at Rome he obtained from him a recognition of the papal claims over Romagna and the Marches. He manœuvred to bring about a pacification between the Guelfs and Ghibellines both at Bologna and at Florence. Unhappily the shortness of his reign prevented him from completing his policy and witnessing its results. After his death Charles determined to secure himself against the recurrence of a similar risk. He took the election into his own hands, won over the friends and adherents of the last pope, and obtained the elevation to the papal throne of a Frenchman devoted to his interests, Simon de Brie, who took the name of Martin IV. This election consolidated the predominance of Charles over the whole of Italy. The Italian towns were filled with French troops. Charles resided with the pope at Viterbo, and never let him out of his sight. At this moment, when at the height of his power, he was preparing to conquer Constantinople, his authority received a blow from an obscure hand.

The throne of Sicily, as has been already mentioned, was claimed by Peter of Arragon, who had married Contanza, the daughter of Manfred. A certain John of Procida, a noble of Salerno, who had been the physician, confidant, and friend of Frederick II. and Manfred, and had supported the enterprise of Conradin, had retired to the Court of Arragon after the battle of Tagliacozzo. From the year 1279 onwards he devoted himself to the double task of wreaking vengeance upon Charles and of establishing the daughter of Manfred in her rights. He first went to Sicily, where he found everything prepared to favour his enterprise. The island, which had taken the side of Manfred against Charles, was kept down by French soldiers with every species of brutality. John advised them to wait for the fitting moment of revenge. He then passed on to Constantinople, where he warned the Greek emperor of the danger which awaited him, and engaged him to assist the king of Arragon with money, in order that he might make a diversion in his favour. As, however, Palæologus refused to do anything without the consent of Pope Nicholas III., John of Procida contrived to obtain this, and had just carried back to Barcelona the news of the success of his mission when he was informed of the sudden death of the pope. Although, as might have been expected, an embassy from Arragon was coldly received by Martin IV., John of Procida did not lose hope. He obtained money from Palæologus, and persuaded Peter to prepare an expedition to be used ostensibly against Africa, from which it might, at any time, be ready to cross over to Sicily, while he himself went to that island to foment the general discontent. The massacre of the Sicilian Vespers, which was the result of these long efforts, took place on Easter Monday, March 30, 1282. The whole population of Palermo was on that day on the road to Monreale to hear vespers in the magnificent church of the monastery. A French soldier had the rashness to insult a beautiful girl under pretence of searching for arms. The cry of "*Muoiano i Francesi*,"—"Death to the French," was raised on all sides, and every Frenchman on the ground was killed. Four thousand persons were put to death on this night; men, women, and children were indiscriminately murdered. The whole of Sicily was in revolt, and Peter of Arragon was invited to assume the crown. He disembarked at

Trapani on August 30, just four months after the massacre. The fleet of Charles was destroyed before his eyes by one of Peter's admirals. The two rivals determined to settle their quarrel by an appeal to the fortune of arms, a curious sign of the times. They agreed to meet at Bordeaux, on May 15, 1283, and to fight against each other, each at the head of a hundred knights. Sicily was to remain the prize of the conqueror; the wishes of the population were regarded as immaterial. The king of England was to guarantee the security of the place of conflict. Edward refused to give the guarantee demanded. Charles appeared at Bordeaux at the time appointed. It is uncertain whether Peter ever came there or not, but, at any rate, he declined to fight. Two months before he had been deposed by the authority of the pope, not only from the kingdom of Sicily, but also from the throne of Arragon, which was given to Charles of Valois, second son of Philippe le Hardi. The last years of the life of Charles of Anjou were clouded with misfortune. During his absence from Naples, his eldest son was taken prisoner by Roger de Loria, grand admiral of Sicily, and the fickle people of Naples proposed to transfer their allegiance to the king of Arragon. Charles returned in time to prevent this from taking effect, but the shock of ingratitude embittered his last moments. The year 1285 witnessed the death of the principal potentates who had been engaged in the struggle which has been narrated. Charles of Anjou died on January 7. Philippe le Hardi, who was engaged in conquering Arragon for his son Charles, died after an unfortunate campaign, at Perpignan on October 6. Peter of Arragon succumbed, on October 6, to wounds received in the same expedition; and in the meantime, Pope Martin IV., the creature of Charles, had expired at Perugia on March 25.

CHAPTER IV.

PISA AND GENOA—CONSTITUTION OF FLORENCE— POPE CELESTINE V.

WHILST the events which have been described in the previous chapter were taking place in the south of Italy, the maritime city of Pisa was reaching the culmination of power which preceded its rapid fall. The town is a well-known place of pilgrimage to Italian travellers, and preserves at the same time memories both of its greatness and of its decline. The city is shrunken into a very small space compared with the limits which it once occupied, but it offers to our admiration four of the most perfect monuments of early Gothic art. The cathedral, built of black and white marble, large and admirably proportioned, a gem in perfect preservation, is raised on its marble platform, open and visible to all. At a little distance rises the baptistery containing the large marble basin used for the blessing of holy water, and the baptism of all the children of the surrounding districts; as well as the pulpit of Nicholas of Pisa, the earliest master of Tuscan sculpture, who founded the school which produced Donatello, Luca della Robbia, Ghiberti, and Michael Angelo. On the other side of the cathedral is seen the circular campanile or bell tower, surrounded by its light arcades, tier above tier, exquisite in lightness and symmetry, made more strange but not more beautiful by the slope which it has taken from the sinking of the soil. At the side of these marvels of design lies the Campo Santo, or burial-ground, a quiet cloister enclosed with Gothic arches, the centre filled with sacred earth from Gethsemane, the wall covered with frescoes by Benozzo, Gozzoli, and Orcagna. Here are buried the illustrious dead of Pisa; here is deposited in an old Roman sarcophagus, the body of Henry of Luxemburg, whose career will claim our attention further on. The town is still watered by the Arno, a statelier stream than when it flows through Florence, deep, and navigable by seaworthy gallies. But the old port is silted up, and grass grows in the deserted streets. The curse of Dante, who prayed that the island of Gorgona might dam up the mouth of the river, has been fulfilled. Even the delicate invalids who, a hundred years ago, found in Pisa an agreeable and bracing air, now go to Cannes, Mentone, and San Remo. The town exists on memories alone.

In 1280 Pisa was the sovereign city of a wide domain. Her territory along the coast extended from the marshes of the Maremma on the south to the Gulf of Spezzia on the north, where it met with the hostile power of Genoa. Pisa possessed nearly the whole of Sardinia, Corsica, and Elba. The position of Corsica was peculiar. That island is divided into two parts by a very high range of mountains, whose summits rival the loftiest peaks of the Apennines. At a time when all communication was effected by sea, the two sides of the island knew very little about each other. They stood, as it were, back to back, one half owning allegiance to Ajaccio, the other to Bastia; the western half dependent on Genoa, the eastern to Pisa. Besides these possessions Pisa had factories at St Jean d'Acre and at

Constantinople. The weakness of Pisa consisted in the plain which lay behind it. That was occupied by a number of hostile towns—Lucca, Florence, Arezzo—always ready to take advantage of a moment of misfortune. Genoa, on the other hand, her victorious rival, was backed by the ridge of the impassable Apennines. The *cornice* or narrow ledge of coast road between Genoa and Spezzia, offered points of vantage for many a little town, which owed allegiance to her proud mistress, but to no one else. The busy ports were well suited for shipbuilding; the sea supplied the wealth and sustenance which the hills denied. Every village sent forth its contingent of hardy sailors, no unworthy fellow-countrymen of Columbus. For these reasons the contest between the two cities was unequal, and the issue could not be doubtful.

Their rivalry, after continuing for a long time, sometimes after the manner of a tournament, with elaborate displays of force, and a chivalrous indifference to secrecy of preparation, terminated in a great disaster. On August 6, 1284, was fought the great battle of Meloria, in which the Pisans were entirely defeated. The fleets of the two cities met in seeming equality, and the accounts of the battle in their minuteness of detail, and their painful insistance on individual disaster, remind us of the terrible defeat of the Athenians in the great harbour of Syracuse as narrated by Thucydides. Galley contended with galley, and man with man. There was no smoke to obscure the horrors of the fight. At length, when the fortune of the battle was wavering, thirty Genoese galleys, which had been concealed behind the Island of Meloria hastened to the attack, and rendered the result no longer doubtful. Five thousand Pisans were slain, eleven thousand were taken prisoners, of whom only one thousand returned at the conclusion of peace fifteen years afterwards. Pisa never recovered the blow, the source of her noble families was dried at its fountain-head. The towns of Tuscany seized the opportunity to complete her destruction. Florence, Lucca, Siena, Pistoia, Prato, Volterra, San Gimignano and Colle signed an alliance with Genoa for the destruction of their common enemy. This calamity was averted by the diplomatic skill of Count Ugolino della Gherardesca who by persuasion and bribery sowed dissension amongst the members of the league. The count was afterwards imprisoned with his sons and grandsons by Archbishop Roger in the *torre della fame* "the tower of hunger." The key was thrown into the Arno, and they were left to perish. The narratives of this horrible deed of vengeance form one of the most thrilling episodes in the Hell of Dante.

We must now turn our attention to the affairs of Florence, the city of Dante himself. It has been stated above that in the year 1250, after the death of Frederick II., the *primo popolo*, that is, the upper middle classes, who formed a commercial aristocracy, began to raise its head, and to assert itself against the nobility. This party deposed the existing *podestà* and appointed some new officers, thirty-six *caporali* or heads chosen from the six divisions of the city, a *capitano del popolo*, or captain of the people, and twelve anziani, or "ancients," to serve as his council. In each ward was organized a company of trained bands, each under his own standard-bearer, while to the captain of the people was entrusted the *gonfalone del popolo*, the standard of the people, half-white and half-red. The towers of the nobles were reduced in height so as to be no longer formidable. From this time, the *capitano*, who was required to be a foreign knight and a doctor of law, stood by the side of the *podestà* as the defender of the people. This change of constitution was a decidedly Guelphic movement, and contributed to the supremacy of that party until its defeat at the battle of Montaperti in 1260.

After this defeat Florence suffered less than might have been expected. Various devices were invented with a view of holding the balance between the two parties. The office of *podestà* was committed to two *frati godenti* from Bologna, who were supposed to belong, one to the Guelph, and the other to the Ghibelline party. This order had been founded in 1233 to appease the strife between Guelphs and Ghibellines. They appointed thirty-six *buonuomini* or overseers, chosen from both parties, to assist them. The guild of *calimala*, the makers of fine Italian cloth, took the lead in the state. Under the protection of the *buonuomini* arose the organisation of arts or guilds, which have been already mentioned above. These guilds were organised with *capitudini* or heads, and *collegi* or assessors, and with captains of companies with the right to banners and soldiers of their own. Besides the twelve guilds, seven of the greater trades and five of the lesser, nine industries of still lower rank strove for recognition at a later period. The final result of these popular or quasi-popular reforms was to re-establish the supremacy of the Guelphs. An institution called the *capitani di parte Guelfa* was formed, consisting of three persons. Their original duty was to manage the confiscated property of Ghibellines, but they afterwards assumed very large political power. The seignory of Florence was committed to King Charles of Anjou for ten years. All Tuscany became Guelph except Pisa and Siena. We have seen above that popes Gregory and Nicholas were not very anxious for the aggrandisement of Charles's power. To carry out their ideas they attempted to effect a new arrangement between Guelph and Ghibelline. Fourteen *buonuomini* were appointed by Pope Nicholas in 1280 to form the *signoria*, and they consisted of eight Guelphs and six Ghibellines. But the arrangement only lasted for two years. In 1282 a final constitution was made, which continued till the close of the liberties of Florence. The *signoria* was made to consist of six *priori*, chosen from the higher guilds, holding office for two months only. They were obliged to lodge and have their meals in one house, to hold no discussion with any one except in a public audience, and were never to leave the city. Some changes were subsequently made in the number of these *priori*; they varied from six to twelve, and when the six wards were replaced by four quarters, became eight in number. The method of these elections was often changed at different times, but the principal object of the several arrangements was to prevent family influence or jobbery. This constitution possessed something of an oligarchical character, being directed on the one hand against the *grandi* or nobles, who could not be elected to the office unless they were members of the guilds, and on the other hand, against the *popolo minuto*, or lower class, who were, however, at first content to be governed by their wealthier fellow-subjects. Power was thus concentrated in the hands of the upper middle class, the rich merchants. These arrangements were not sufficient to keep the *grandi* in check, and their feuds were the occasion of perpetual disturbance.

In order to put an end to these quarrels the *ordinamenta justitiæ*, the ordinances of justice, were passed by the Popolani under Giano della Bella in 1292, he being a man of noble family, who had been included in the guilds. The general effect of these regulations was that the fact of being a *grande* was an incapacity for holding office, and to be made a *grande* was one of the penalties with which prominent citizens were visited by their political enemies. The severest penalties were inflicted on a *grande* who wounded a citizen; the *grandi* were excluded from all places and offices, except by the consent of the commune, and from the registers of the citizens, between the ages of sixteen and seventy. They could not accuse nor bear witness nor appear in court against *popolani* without consent of the *priori*. They were also not allowed to live within one hundred and fifty ells of a bridge. To aid in the execution of these laws a *Gonfaloniere della giustizia*, or standard-bearer of justice, was appointed. He was to be a member of one of the superior guilds, to have a vote with the priors, and not to belong to any house from which any of the priors came. The office was to last for two months, and to be filled by persons chosen from the six wards of the city successively. This important functionary had in his charge the *gonfalone*, or standard of the people, and had under him a body of chosen foot soldiers, first one thousand in number, then increased to two thousand, and in 1295 to four thousand. Similar arrangements were made in the districts around Florence, so that a militia was was always ready to crush any uprising on the part of the nobles.

It is interesting to remember that the great poet Dante, who was born in 1265, possibly took part in these constitutional changes, and that Brunetto Latini, his preceptor, was *notaio del commune*, or town clerk. It is also probable that Dante fought in the battle of Campaldino on June 11, 1289—a battle in which the Ghibelline inhabitants of Arezzo

were entirely defeated, but which did not enable the united
armies of Florence and Siena to take the town.

Before we pursue the interior history of Florence further
we must turn our attention to the events which were taking
place at this time in the other parts of Italy. Pope Martin
IV., the creature of Charles of Anjou, was succeeded by two
Popes who were indeed Italians, but who had no influence
either on Italian or on European history. Pope Honorius
IV., of the illustrious family of Savelli, was unable to pray or
to celebrate mass, or to perform the most ordinary ecclesiastical duties without mechanical aid. He reigned for two
years, from 1285 to 1287. Nicholas IV., his successor, is
chiefly known for his subservience to the interests of the
noble family of Colonna. He died in 1292. After his
death there was a vacancy of the Holy See for more than
two years. This interregnum resulted in the election of a
Pope whose life and reign is too characteristic of the middle
ages not to claim our attention.

The city of Sulmona, the birthplace of the poet Ovid, is
situated in one of the wildest and most romantic districts of
Italy. It lies at the extremity of that great central valley
of which we have before spoken, in which were founded
Corfinium the capital of the Sammite league and Aquila, the
capital of the Emperor Frederick II. It is a cold and bleak
region, chilled by the eternal snows of the mighty peaks of
the Gran Sasso d' Italia and the Matese. In a cavern
hollowed out of the steep rock, not far from Sulmona, had
lived for many years an aged hermit, Pietro di Morone.
His body was wasted with privations and tortures worthy
of an Indian Fakir, but the reputation of his sanctity had
spread far and near, and his wild utterances were taken as
the words of prophetic inspiration. By a sudden impulse

the College of Cardinals determined to elect this holy man as pope. He ran away from the deputation sent to do him reverence, but was caught and detained by main force, and conducted to the cathedral of Aquila, in which he was to receive the papal crown. It is difficult to account for his election. Perhaps the College of Cardinals, weary of perpetual intrigue, determined to remit their cause into the hands of God, and to raise to the headship of Christendom the holiest and most saint-like man they knew. The cathedral of Aquila is one of the most perfect specimens of the Italian Gothic of the time of Frederick II. It is said that the door by which the new Pope entered has never been opened since, and certainly the carved ornaments which surround it are as fresh as on the day when they were first sculptured. As he rode through the streets of Aquila his bridle was held by two kings, Charles II. of Naples, the son of Charles of Anjou, who had been liberated from prison by the Arragonese, and his son Charles Martel, king of Hungary, who had acquired that title by his marriage with the heiress to the Hungarian crown. The new Pontiff assumed the name of Celestine V. Whatever may have been the motives for his election, it could not have resulted in a greater failure. He was entirely unfit for the most ordinary matters of business. He gave away the same benefice to different people ; he scattered indulgences with the most lavish hand ; he kept four lenten seasons in the year instead of one, and during these periods was absolutely invisible ; worse than all, he was completely in the power of the Angevin kings. Charles persuaded him to create twelve non-Italian cardinals, of whom seven were French, and this act of weakness was the final cause of the transference of the papal see to Avignon.

At last, on December 13, 1294, he resigned the pontificate with the consent of the cardinals. Ten days later a successor was elected in the person of Benedetto Gaetani, who took the name of Boniface VIII.

Celestine had up to the time of his abdication resided at Naples, but Boniface compelled him to accompany him to Rome. On the road thither he escaped, and took refuge in the hermitage in which he had spent so many years. Dragged from this by force, he sought a refuge in the forests of Apulia, and eventually embarked on board ship with the intention of crossing the Adriatic. Driven back to the coast by a storm, he was seized by the emissaries of Boniface, and was at last immured in the castle of Fumone, which stands on the summit of a lofty rock not far from the valley of the Liris. Here he was treated with the most cruel rigour. He was allowed to see no one except a few hermits of his own order, and in this prison he died on May 19, 1296, twenty-two months after his election. It is believed that Dante alludes to him as one "who made the great refusal," placing him in the most despicable part of the Inferno, amongst the cowards who did neither good nor harm in life, as a punishment for having renounced the great office of reforming the Church of God. However this may be, his history should be to us rather significant of the sharp antagonism which existed between the church and the world in the thirteenth century. It shows us how ascetic and self-devoted piety, while able to influence the mass of the people, and to excite the hopes and enthusiasm of some of those who were in high places, yet when brought into conflict with the passions so fiercely raging in the world, earned for its possessor nothing but a life of torture and a death of ignominy. In happier days an ascetic life would be less wildly eccentric, and, at the same time, would not be denied its influence over the affairs of men.

Important changes were now taking place in the government of Italy, Spain, and France, which had a serious influence over the fortunes of the Italian peninsula. Philippe le Hardi, king of France, who died in 1285, was succeeded by his son Philippe le Bel. His second son was Charles of Valois, who had been invested by Pope Martin IV. with the crown of Arragon. In 1288 Edward I., king of England, had made peace between Naples, France, and Arragon, on the following terms. Charles II. was to be liberated from prison, and to be recognised as king of Naples. James of Arragon, brother of Alfonso, king of Arragon, who had succeeded Peter of Arragon in 1285, was to be recognised as king of Sicily. Charles II. was to persuade his cousin, Charles of Valois, to surrender his rights to the crown of Arragon, receiving a compensation of 20,000 pounds of silver. This treaty, however, came to nothing. Charles II. was crowned by Pope Nicholas IV., king of the two Sicilies, and Charles of Valois refused to complete his renunciation, and, on the contrary, allied himself with Sancho, king of Castile, with the view of attacking that kingdom. Alfonso, forced to submission, agreed to surrender, as far as in him lay, the kingdom of Sicily to Charles II., on the condition that Charles of Valois gave up his pretensions to the throne of Arragon. Shortly after this Alfonso died, and was succeeded by his brother James, who in his turn left the kingdom of Sicily to his brother Frederick. Thus Sicily lay as a bone of contention between France and Spain, the population, as before, loathing the idea of submission to the rule of the French. Boniface VIII., on his election to the papacy, endeavoured to reconcile these conflicting elements. He proposed that James of Arragon should marry Blanche of Naples, daughter of Charles II., with a large dowry, receiving also Corsica and Sardinia, which belonged at that time to Pisa and Genoa, the Pope considering that he was paramount lord of all islands, and might give them to whom he pleased. In return for this addition to his dominions James was to surrender Sicily to Charles II. James was quite willing to assent to this treaty, but his brother Frederick, the actual ruler of Sicily, had to be dealt with. He was offered as a bribe to marry Catherine, grand-daughter and heir of Baldwin II., Emperor of Constantinople, receiving a large sum of money to assist him in conquering this new empire. John of Procida and Roger di Loria, veteran patriots of the Spanish cause, dissuaded him from accepting this tempting offer. When James attempted to stand by the promise he had given, the Sicilian barons renounced their allegiance to him and recognised his brother Frederick as king. Thus the war went on between the French and the Arragonese in Calabria and Sicily, and James was compelled to take part against his own brother. For some years he assisted Charles II. against him, but gave up the contest for very shame in 1299. Charles of Valois, who had entered Tuscany in 1301, sailed for Sicily in 1302. He had, however, but little success, and soon concluded peace. The conditions were that Frederick was to marry Eleanora, daughter of Charles II., to retain Sicily during his life, with the title of king of Trinacria, with the promise that after his death the island should pass to the house of Anjou. This event did not, however, take place till the year 1337, and before that time the relations of the chief actors in the drama towards each other had become materially changed.

CHAPTER V.

BLACKS AND WHITES—CHARLES OF VALOIS—REMOVAL
OF POPES TO AVIGNON.

ALTHOUGH the political character of Florence had now
become principally Guelph, the spirit of faction was far
from being appeased. As in other Italian towns, political
parties gradually lost their original meaning, and degener-
ated into mere personal quarrels, being inherited by generation after generation like a Corsican *vendetta*. The Guelphs,
when left to themselves as the masters of Florence, split up
into two parties, the Bianchi and Neri, the Whites and the
Blacks. This division, besides its intrinsic importance in
the history of the city, claims especial interest from its connection with the fortunes of the poet Dante. The evil of
party faction was not indigenous to Florence. It was
caught like a plague from the neighbouring city of Pistoia,
always celebrated for the violence of its revolutions. Here
two families were at constant war with each other, like the
Montagues and Capulets in the Verona of Shakespeare.
The Cancellieri were at the head of the Guelphs, and the
Panciatichi of the Ghibellines. In the general preponderance of the Guelph party throughout the valley of the
Arno, the Cancellieri had driven out their rivals and taken
possession of the town. This family, excluded, it is true,
from office, but very rich and powerful, became divided,

owing to a domestic quarrel, into two factions, the Bianchi
and the Neri. The safety of the whole town was en-
dangered by their reckless strife. A fear arose lest the
exiled Ghibellines might seize their opportunity of returning. So the *signoria* of the city was entrusted to the
Florentines, and the heads of the two parties were ordered
to leave Pistoia, and to take up their abode in the sovereign
city. This measure was followed by the most disastrous
consequences. Florence was just beginning to prosper
under its new constitution. The magnificent Palazzo
Pubblico was rising in the great square, and a larger
circuit than before was being enclosed by a coronet of
walls. But under this appearance of peace, the quarrel
between the *grandi* and the *popolani* was ready to break
out. The two principal rival families in Florence were the
Donati and the Cerchi, one representing the old nobility,
the other the new families enriched by commerce. Corso
Donati was at the head of one, Vieri de Cerchi at the head
of the other. On the arrival of the exiles from Pistoia, the
Whites received the favour of the Cerchi, the Blacks of the
Donati, and their names were quickly transferred to the
factions at Florence. The Bianchi rather favoured the side
of the Ghibellines, the Neri that of the Guelphs. The
Bianchi contained at this time probably the most distinguished men in Florence—Dante, Guido Cavalcanti, and
Dino Compagni. As has been before remarked, they em-
braced the Ghibelline cause not because they were indifferent to Italian liberties, or because they thought lightly
of the danger of German domination, but because they saw
the need of a strong hand to control the factions of their
distracted country. They felt keenly the mischief of the
temporal power of the Church, and they had no faith in any

salvation which was to be effected by the intervention of France.

The struggle between these two parties lasted just two years, as the Pistoians were received into Florence in the spring of 1300, and the Whites were finally expelled from the city in April 1302.

Pope Boniface VIII. attempted to make peace. In June 1300 he sent Cardinal Aquasparta to Florence to reconcile the two factions, and to draw up a scheme for dividing the government between them. The Whites, who had the upper hand, refused to accede to the arrangement, and the Cardinal went away in a rage, having placed the city under an interdict. The priors, left to themselves, ordered the chiefs of the two parties to quit the town. The Blacks were sent to Castel della Pieve, in the neighbourhood of Perugia, the Whites to Sarzana, a town in the northern Apennines on the road to Parma. The rivals were thus divided by the whole extent of the territory of the republic. Guido Cavalcanti was one of the exiled Whites, and it is probable that Dante, his devoted friend, was one of the priors who pronounced sentence against him. Sarzana was found to be unhealthy. Guido Cavalcanti fell ill; the Whites were allowed to return, but Guido died almost immediately afterwards at the beginning of 1301. Corso Donati, the head of the Black party, now went to Rome, and persuaded the pope to take more rigorous measures to reduce Florence to obedience. The eyes of Boniface were naturally turned towards France, and especially to Charles of Valois, the son of Philippe le Hardi, and the brother of Philippe le Bel, who had several reasons to draw him towards Italy. He had, as we have seen, been invested by Pope Martin IV. with the kingdom of Arragon, and had attempted to obtain this possession by force of arms. Also his cousin, Charles II. of Naples, the son and successor of Charles of Anjou, was struggling with Frederick of Arragon for the possession of Sicily. Charles of Valois was not disposed to reject the overtures of the Pope, not only from family reasons, but because Charles II. had been promised the crown of Sicily as part of his treaty with James of Arragon. Boniface offered him the hand of Catherine, Princess of Constantinople, which had been refused by Frederick of Arragon, and even held out hopes of advancement to the Imperial crown of Germany.

It would have perhaps been wise to have opposed his advance in the passes of the Apennines, but the Whites shrank from declaring themselves so decidedly in the Ghibelline cause. Charles first marched southwards to Siena, then in the autumn retraced his steps towards the north, and entered Florence on November 1, 1301. But on the one side there was weakness, and on the other breach of faith. The Cerchi were either too timid or too trusting. Charles, under a show of impartiality, could not avoid a feeling of tenderness towards the Blacks. Corso Donati was admitted into the town. The priors were driven from power. For five days the city was given up to pillage and fire. Charles remained indifferent to the disorders which were taking place, and affected to observe nothing. On November 11, new priors and a new gonfaloniere were elected, all of the Black party. Cante de' Gabrielli da Gubbio was invested with the office of *podestà*. In five months he condemned six hundred persons to exile. Amongst these was the poet Dante, who was then absent from Florence, perhaps on an embassy to Pope Boniface at Rome. The whole city was now completely in the hands of the Blacks. On April 4, 1302, Charles of Valois, gorged with the plunder of the city which he had come to pacify, left for his Sicilian expedition, of which an account has been given in the previous chapter.

The condition of Florence was no better than before. The struggle was now between the *grandi* of the *parte nera*, under Corso Donati, and the *popolani* of the same party. In March 1304 Cardinal da Prato attempted to make peace, but with little effect. On June 10 of the same year there was a battle between the *grandi* and the *popolani* in the streets. In July the Whites, under Vieri de' Cerchi, made a vigorous effort to return to their native city. They forced their way into the town as far as the Piazza di San Marco, but were there repulsed. In 1306 the office of *esecutore* was instituted to keep down the *grandi*. Finally on September 15, 1308, Corso Donati was expelled from the city, and was killed in his flight. In this year the election of Henry of Luxemburg to the imperial crown gave new hopes for the peace of Florence and of Italy.

Events now entered upon a new phase by the outbreak of a violent dispute between Boniface VIII. and the king of France. Under the pretence of a personal quarrel lay the desire of the French people to found a Gallican, that is, a national Church. The Pope had attempted to exercise over Philippe le Bel a kind of tutelage, which since the days of Innocent III. had been frequently arrogated by popes who possessed any unusual strength of character. Boniface had ordered Philip to release Guy, Count of Flanders, from prison, and to make peace with England. He had created a new bishopric at Pamiers, and had made the bishop, whom he consecrated to the see, apostolical legate in France. He had also claimed the right of deciding whether the French clergy should or should not pay taxes to the king. On the other hand, the king had intercepted

the revenue which the Pope received from France, and had
thrown the Bishop of Pamiers into prison.   The king hoped
that he would be supported by his States General in asserting
the royal authority against that of the Pope.   Before this
quarrel broke out Boniface had persecuted the noble family
of Colonna, and some members of this family had taken
refuge at Paris to demand vengeance.   The French clergy
responded to the summons of their king.   They sent letters
to the Pope in 1302, in which they denied his right to regu-
late the taxes imposed by the crown, to forbid the king to
imprison a bishop, or to assume an authority over the king's
conscience.   The French nobles took a stronger line than
the clergy.   On March 12, 1301, William of Nogaret
accused Boniface of simony, heresy, magic, and other
crimes, and called for a general council to depose him from
the papal see.   Boniface, in his turn, summoned the French
clergy to meet at Rome to discuss the reformation of the
kingdom of France.   Philip ordered them not to obey
the summons, and Boniface replied by excommunicating
Philip by the bull *Ausculta fili*.   The bull was publicly
burned in Paris, and the three estates of the realm,
assembled in Nôtre Dame, assured the king of the support of his people.   William of Nogaret now took the
quarrel into his own hands. Accompanied by Sciarra
Colonna and other enemies of Boniface, he set out
for Rome.   On September 7, 1303, he arrived at Anagni,
the native town of Boniface, where he held his court.   No
resistance was made.   The knights spread themselves over
the palace, and plundered as they pleased.   The old man,
now eighty years of age, like another Becket, dressed himself in his pontifical robes and knelt before the altar.   The
knights did not dare to lay hands on the Vicar of Christ.

For three days the pope remained a prisoner, until at last the populace of Anagni rose in indignation, drove away the foreign knights, and released the holy father. Boniface did not long survive this insult. He proceeded to Rome, and took refuge with the Orsini, the ancestral enemies of the Colonna. Believing himself to be again a prisoner, he attempted to remove from the Vatican to the Lateran palace, but the Orsini refused to let him go. He locked himself up in his chamber, and was found dead by his attendant, his hair clotted with blood, as if he had dashed his head against the wall. Then on October 12, 1303, was the persecution of Celestine V. avenged.

Immediately after the death of Boniface VIII. the cardinals made choice of an excellent pope, who took the name of Benedict XI. He attempted to set himself free from the tyranny of the cardinals and of the Orsini and the Colonna, who were supreme at Rome. Notwithstanding their resistance, he succeeded in removing his court to Perugia. He had, however, immediately to deal with the difficulty of reconciling his duty to the memory of Boniface with the friendship of the Court of France. On the one hand, he could not leave the insults inflicted on his predecessor unavenged ; on the other hand, he did not wish to involve himself in a serious quarrel with Philip. He tried to pursue a middle course by summoning William of Nogaret and fourteen other nobles, chiefly Italians, by name, to appear before him at Rome. He added to these, without special mention, those who had contributed to the crime. Philip believed that he was included in this denunciation, and therefore took care that Benedict should be poisoned in a dish of figs. He died on July 4, 1304.

The events which followed this murder led to the trans-

ference of the papal see to Avignon in France, the so-called
Babylonian captivity, which did not finally come to an end
until the return of Pope Gregory XI. to Italy in the year
1377. For ten months the cardinals shut up in Perugia
could not agree on the choice of a pope. They were
divided into two evenly balanced factions—the Guelphs,
headed by the Orsini; and the Ghibellines, headed by the
Colonna. At last the citizens of Perugia starved them into
a settlement by diminishing their rations, and the two
parties came to a strange agreement. They at first determined that no Italian should be elected. It was next
arranged that the Orsini should nominate three candidates,
of whom one should be finally chosen by the Colonna.
The Orsini took care to nominate only such men as should
be hostile to Philippe le Bel. Among them was Bertrand de Gotte, Archbishop of Bordeaux, who was believed to be a deadly enemy both of Philip and of Charles
of Valois. Philip was immediately informed of what had
happened, and his action has passed into the following
legend. He travelled rapidly into Gascony, met the
Archbishop, and proposed terms of reconciliation. They
heard mass together, and the king said: "Archbishop, I
have it in my power to make you pope, and if you will
promise six things, I will raise you to that dignity." Bertrand assented, and the king proceeded to declare his six
conditions:—1. That when made pope he should readmit
him into the church and pardon his conduct to Pope
Boniface; 2. That he would admit the king and his
friends to communion with the church; 3. That he would
grant him the tithes of the clergy for five years, to cover the
expenses of the war with Flanders; 4. That he would
destroy and blot out the memory of Pope Boniface; 5.

That he would restore the dignity of Cardinal to James and Peter Colonna; 6. That he would grant him another great favour, of which he would tell him in due time and place. The Archbishop swore upon the book that he would perform what he was asked, and gave his brother and two of his nephews to the king as hostages. The king then promised to make him pope. This story, originally related by Giovanni Villani, has been shown by recent criticism to be untrue.

It can easily be understood why Clement V., for that was the title of the new pope, had no desire to visit Italy. He was afraid of the vengeance of those whom he had deceived, and he was too valuable to the king of France to be readily parted with. He was indeed a considerable source of income to the French monarch; he allowed the king to tax his clergy; he gave permission to the Court of Flanders to do the same in order to pay tribute to the crown of France; and he gave Philip authority to expel all Jews from his dominions and to confiscate their property. Clement was crowned at Lyons on the day of St Martin, November 11, 1305, in the presence of Philippe le Bel, Charles of Valois, and a number of Italian princes. He shortly afterwards created twelve cardinals, the two Colonnas and ten Frenchmen devoted to the interests of the French crown. He fixed the papal see at Avignon on the Rhine, where the pope presented a small territory acquired by confiscations from the Albigensian heretics.

Of the six promises which Clement is said to have made to the king, he had already performed the first, second, third, and fifth. There remained the condemnation of Pope Boniface and the granting of the secret request, the terms of which had not as yet been made known. Although strongly pressed by the king, Clement could not bring himself to condemn his predecessor, or to declare him guilty of heresy; to do this would be to nullify the appointment of the very cardinals by whom Benedict XI. and Clement himself had been elected. He therefore remitted the question to a General Council. On the other hand, on June 1, 1307, he issued a bull which gave the most complete absolution to the king, together with his agents and all those who were in any way compromised by ecclesiastical censures. William of Nogaret, who was said to have struck the aged pontiff with his hand, and Reginald Cupino were alone exempted, and were ordered to undertake a pilgrimage to the Holy Land. An Œcumenical Council was summoned to meet at Vienne on October 1, 1310. There is no doubt that the secret request which Philip reserved *in petto* was the suppression of the Order of the Templars. This Order had been founded in 1126 by nine French knights who accompanied Godefroi de Bouillon to the Holy Land. Just at this time the Templars, with their grand master Jacques de Molay, had retired to Cyprus on being driven out of Palestine by the Turks. De Molay was recalled from the East, the Templars were imprisoned, and many of them were put to death with the greatest torture. The Council of Vienne abolished the Order in 1311, and transferred its property to the Knights Hospitallers of St John. There is little doubt that the principal motive of Philip in these acts of violence was to enrich himself by confiscating the property of the Order. Jacques de Molay was burned on March 12, 1314, and with his dying breath summoned both pope and king to appear before the tribunal of heaven within a year and a day.

By the removal of the Pope to Avignon the condition of

the States of the Church was greatly altered. Bologna became a republic; Ravenna fell under the power of the family of Polenta; Rimini submitted itself to the Malatesta; Urbino to the Montefeltri. Rome underwent various fortunes, among which was the establishment of a republic by Rienzi; while to the south of Rome the principality of Beneventum dared to raise its head. During the immediate course of this history it will be necessary to remember that these cities owe much of their importance in the varying fortunes of the peninsula to the absence of that power which formerly kept them in subjection to a common authority.

CHAPTER VI.

ADOLF OF NASSAU—HENRY OF LUXEMBURG—VENICE.

RUDOLF of Hapsburg, Emperor of Germany, died on July
15, 1291. He was succeeded by Adolf of Nassau, a
prince of a comparatively poor house in the neighbourhood
of the Rhine. Adolf was crowned at Aix-la-Chapelle, on
June 24, 1292, but exactly six years afterwards was deposed. The electors called the people together and proclaimed that the king had rejected the counsels of the
wise and acquiesced in those of the young men, and had
never fulfilled the duties of a ruler; also, that he had no
wealth of his own, or friends who would help him faithfully.
Seeing these defects, and more than twenty others, they
had asked, and, so they said, obtained the Papal permission
to absolve him from the dignity of reigning. Each elector
gave his own reason. One said, "King Adolf is poor in
money and friends, he is a fool, the kingdom under him
will soon fail in wealth and honour;" another said, "It is
necessary that he should be deposed;" another proposed
to choose the Duke of Austria; another said, "The counsel
is sound, let it be done at once." Among the more cir-
cumstantial charges were the following: he had been use-
less and faithless to the interests of the Empire, he had
neglected Italy and the outlying provinces, he had failed to
maintain the peace, and had allowed and encouraged
private war, he had neglected good counsel, despised the

clergy, contemned the nobles and preferred mere knights in their place, and had served as a mercenary in the armies of Edward I. of England.[1] His successor was Albert, Duke of Austria, son of the Emperor Rudolf. He was nominated concurrently with the deposition of his predecessor, and was crowned at Aix-la-Chapelle, on August 24, 1294. Adolf did not give way without a struggle, but was killed in the battle of Gollheim, near Worms.

Albert did not pay any greater attention to the affairs of Italy than his predecessor had done. The Ghibellines of the type of Dante, who sought in the power of the emperor the best means of appeasing the factions of their country, looked to him in vain. Dante cries out indignantly in the Purgatory (vi. 97), "O, Albert of Germany, thou who abandoned her who has turned untamable and savage, whereas it was thy duty to vault into the saddle, may a righteous judgment fall upon thy race from heaven, and may it be new and clear to all men so that thy successor may dread it for himself, for thou and thy father drawn aside to the north of the Alps by your cupidity, have allowed the garden of the Empire to become a desert." Albert was occupied in increasing the possessions of his house, and in trying to extend his authority over the free Cantons of Switzerland, in the north of which lies the old castle of Hapsburg, the cradle of the house of Austria. In his reign took place the patriotic struggle of the Forest Cantons for freedom, which are known to us by the Oath of the Rütli and the mythical exploits of Tell and Gessler. Albert was murdered in 1308, just after crossing the ford of the Reuss, close by the castle of Hapsburg, by his nephew John, whom he had deprived of his possessions.

[1] Stubbs ii. 365.

Philip of France, who had already intimated to Pope Clement that his secret and concealed request had been to fix the seat of the Papacy in France, and to destroy the Templars, now declared that it was to secure the crown of the empire for his brother Charles of Valois. Clement, however, was by this time weary of compliance, and whilst feigning to agree with the King's request, wrote to the electors to hasten their proceedings, and pointed out to them as a desirable candidate Henry, Count of Luxemburg, a prince of little importance and comparatively poor, but well-known to be of chivalrous and noble character. Henry was elected in November 1308, and was recognised by the Pope. He is known in history as Henry VII. of Luxemburg. His son John married Elizabeth of Bohemia, and thus became King of Bohemia. Under this title he fought against Edward III. and the Black Prince at the battle of Crécy, and was there taken prisoner. The three white feathers which formed his emblem, with the motto "Ich dien," still serve as the badge of the Princes of Wales.

Henry, anxious to repair the neglect of his predecessors, determined that an expedition to Italy should form the first business of his reign. In 1310 he received the representatives of the Italian powers at Lausanne on the Lake of Geneva. About the end of September he crossed the Graian Alps and entered Piedmont by the pass of the Mont Cenis. He reached the town of Asti on October 10. Like many others who had set their hands to the pacification of Italy he resolved to make no distinction of parties, but to bring about an understanding between Guelphs and Ghibellines. But it was impossible that he should be regarded by all parties alike. The Ghibelline despots of the cities of the Lombard plain received him with joy, but they were not gratified by the intention which he expressed of recalling the Guelph exiles. On the other hand, the cities of Florence, Siena, Lucca, and Bologna stood aloof from him, and Robert, king of Naples, grandson and successor of Charles II., sent an ambassador to greet him. Pisa welcomed him gladly, the city in which he afterwards found a tomb. With reference to Robert of Naples, it should be mentioned that his grandfather, Charles II., had died on May 5, 1309, Charles Martel, the eldest son of Charles II., had previously succeeded to the throne of his mother Maria, queen of Hungary, or, at least, bore the title from 1290 to 1295, when he died. His son Charles Robert was recognised as his father's heir in 1308, and he was, of course, the legitimate sovereign of Sicily. He had, however, been educated entirely abroad, and Charles II. at his death, in the succeeding year, left the crown to his second son Robert. His title was acknowledged by the Pope, and he reigned as king of Naples, with claims upon Sicily till 1343.

Henry arrived at Milan at the end of December 1310. The city was at this time divided between the two factions of the della Torre and the Visconti, Guido della Torre having for the moment the upper hand. The emperor pursued the same policy of peace which he had before adopted in his own. He ordered that all the exiles should be allowed to return, and that their property should be restored. On January 6, 1311, Henry was crowned with the iron crown of Lombardy in the Church of Sant Ambrogio. The appearance of peace was unfortunately of short duration. The emperor asked the town council for money. Guglielmo da Pusterla proposed a grant of 50,000 gold ducats. Matteo dei Visconti suggested that an additional sum of

10,000 ducats should be added for the emperor. Guido della Torre went beyond this second sum, and said that nothing short of 100,000 ducats was worthy of the wealth and magnificence of the capital of Lombardy. Henry refused to abate any portion of this larger contribution, and proceeded to lay the districts around Milan in a similar proportion. This unfortunate want of money always made the German emperors unpopular in Italy, yet it was not unreasonable that their Italian subjects should contribute to their support. This demand produced a change of government in Milan. The two parties of the Della Torre and the Visconti united to expel the Germans from the city. Henry fortunately heard of the conspiracy before it could be put into execution, and sent to apprehend those who had contrived the treachery. Matteo Visconti, warned in time, received the Emperor's messengers with expressions of courteous friendship, but Della Torre had unluckily gone too far to dissimulate. Matteo joined Henry in taking arms against the rebels. The Torrigiani were driven from the town, but not without much resistance and a murderous struggle. For a moment the cities of the Guelphic league were inspired by Della Torre to throw off their allegiance to the Emperor. Lodi, Crema, and Cremona were soon subdued. Brescia held out a little longer, but was also reduced. When Henry left Lombardy for Genoa he instituted Matteo Visconti as imperial vicar in the city and district of Milan. The city remained subject to his family until they were succeeded by the Sforzas in the middle of the fifteenth century.

The city of Genoa had been torn asunder by the two rival families of Doria and Spinola, the first Guelph, the second Ghibelline. The Doria had at this time just succeeded in getting the upper hand, and peace had been made between the two factions. Henry was received in the "proud city," as Genoa loved to call herself, with every kind of honour, and was made Lord Paramount of the town for twenty years. In return he confirmed the peace which had been auspiciously begun, and on his departure left Uguccione della Faggiuola as imperial vicar. Uguccione governed his charge wisely until the death of the Emperor, when he removed to Pisa, and the troubles, as we shall see, broke out anew. Henry had received at Genoa ambassadors sent somewhat tardily by King Robert of Naples, and there was at this time a faint hope that peace might be secured between the two potentates. Henry had carefully refrained from interfering with those districts of Piedmont which had submitted themselves to the sovereignty of Robert. But the interests of the two sovereigns were completely and radically opposed. As Henry proceeded further in his enterprise he found the hope with which he had commenced it impossible to realise, the chasm between the two parties of Guelph and Ghibelline was too wide to bridge over, and it became more and more necessary for the Emperor to identify himself with that party which had always supported the imperial supremacy, and to crush his adversaries by force. King Robert, on returning from Avignon, where he had gone to be invested with the crown of Naples, stopped for a time at Florence. Here he took counsel as to the best means of opposing the progress of their common enemy. Robert was the nominal head of the Guelphic league, but Florence was the heart and soul of the confederation. It was not without reason that Dante, who was passionately eager for Henry's success, urged

E

the Emperor again and again, with passionate vehemence, to neglect all smaller matters, and to establish his authority by force in that nest of anarchy. The signs of enmity soon became apparent. Henry's ambassadors were refused a passage through Florence, and the Florentine merchants were expelled from Genoa.

Henry set sail from Genoa on February 16, 1312. He was detained for eighteen days at Porto Venere, a picturesque old town situated at the entrance of the Gulf of Spezia. He arrived at Pisa on March 6, and stayed there for six weeks. The Pisans followed the example of the Genoese by investing him with the lordship of their city. They had already presented him with sixty thousand gold ducats, and they now gave him as much again. They hoped that by his assistance Pisa might regain her former position as mistress of Tuscany. Leaving Pisa on April 23, he marched through Siena and Orvieto to Rome. Rome was at this time divided by the Tiber into two hostile camps. The Vatican, the castle of Sant Angelo, and the Leonine city was held by the Orsini and Guelphs; the Coliseum and the Vatican by the Colonna and the Ghibellines. The emperor's advance was opposed at once, he was not permitted to cross the Ponte Molle without a battle. At length the goal of his long pilgrimage was reached, and he was crowned emperor in the church of St John Lateran, on June 29, 1312, the feast of St Peter and St Paul. After the coronation the emperor retired to Tivoli, and many of his German followers returned home. From Tivoli he removed to the strong town of Todi, which he intended to make the base of his operations against Tuscany. Florence had strained every nerve to oppose him. She was in communication with all the Guelphic cities of Italy, she endeavoured to shake the allegiance of Padua and Parma, she negotiated with the courts of Avignon and France. It must be remembered that these vigorous and delicate negotiations were conducted by a government of traders, unskilled in the higher politics, and represented by a ministry which was changed every two months. In August the emperor marched northwards through the territory of Perugia and Arezzo, burning and plundering as he advanced. In Arezzo he was received with joy. In September he marched on Florence, took the towns of Montevarchi and Castel San Giovanni, eluded the Florentine army which was posted at Incisa, and arrived before the gates of the city of flowers, on September 19. He did not dare to attack because he was greatly inferior in force; he allowed the terror inspired by his approach to disappear, and the Florentines received reinforcements from Tuscany and the Romagna. They indeed paid little attention to him, and fortified none of the gates, excepting the one before which he was encamped. He laid waste the territory of Florence till the end of October, and then marched to San Casciano, where he staid till January 6. Finding that pestilence had broken out amongst his troops, he retired to the Castle of Poggibonzi on the road to Siena, and on March 6 returned to Pisa.

The historian, Villani, says of Henry, that he was never cast down by adversity nor unduly elated by prosperity. At Pisa he adopted the best means he could devise for securing the ends he had in view. He held an imperial court, at which he solemnly condemned the Florentines, and took away from them the right of coining money. He deposed Robert, king of Naples, and absolved his subjects from their allegiance. He made an alliance with

Frederick of Arragon, king of Sicily, and sent pressing messages to Germany for a new army. At last, in the beginning of August 1313, after receiving large reinforcements both from Germany and Italy, he felt himself strong enough to take the field against the king of Naples. The Florentines, on their side, conferred the *signoria*, or lordship of their city, on King Robert for five years. The gathering storm was suddenly dispelled by the unexpected death of the Emperor at the monastery of Buonconvento, in the neighbourhood of Siena. The story was long current that he died by receiving the sacrament from a Dominican monk in a poisoned chalice. But he had long been in bad health, and there is nothing strange in his dying of fever in Italy at the end of August. He was buried in the Campo Santo at Pisa. His death closes one of the most romantic episodes to be found in the whole history of mediæval Italy. It also wrought a complete revolution in the affairs of Tuscany. Pisa, with the help of Uguccione della Faggiuola, who had removed to that city from Genoa on the death of his mother, attempted to place himself at the head of the Ghibelline cause, at first with some prospect of success. The first exploit of Uguccione was to capture Lucca; he then laid siege to the castle of Montecatini on the road to Florence, and here, on August 29, 1315, the Florentines were completely defeated. Philip of Tarentum, the eldest son of king Robert of Naples, had been sent to their assistance; his brother Peter, and his son Charles were slain in the battle. In April 1361, Uguccione, whose government had become tyrannical, was turned out both of Lucca and Pisa, and his place was taken by Castruccio Castracani, whose fortunes we shall follow in another place.

The Republic of Venice had remained only an interested

spectator of the events which have been just related. She
sent an ambassador to welcome the Emperor, Henry VII.,
on his arrival in Italy, but, defended by her lagoons, she was
secure against the rivalry of Guelfs and Ghibellines, and
devoted her energies to the extension of her empire in the
east. She underwent, however, important revolutions of her
own. During these years Venice experienced changes in her
internal constitution which gradually made her one of the
strongest oligarchies the world has ever seen. It is the
essence of aristocratic oligarchies, that they have to be
continually on their guard against two opposite dangers—
the degeneration into a democracy, and the concentration
into a monarchy. The similarity between the constitutional histories of Sparta and Venice,—two states so diverse
in origin and in situation—show that these tendencies are
inherent in the character of the state itself, independent of
surrounding circumstances. We have seen, in a previous
chapter, how the power of the Great Council was increased
step by step, how it encroached upon the authority of the
Doge on the one hand, and of the people on the other,
and how its power came gradually to be confined to
the representatives of certain favoured families. In
February 1297, under the Doge Pier Gradenigo, who held
the office from 1289 to 1311, and who was a strong
supporter of the aristocratic party, a law was passed by
which the *quarantia*, a judicial board of forty members,
were to ballot with respect to all those who had been
members of the Great Council within the last four years,
and every one who received at least twelve votes out of
thirty was to be a member for the ensuing year. This
provision, as far as it went, confined admission to the
Great Council exclusively to those families who had been

already elected to it, but the opportunity of infusing new blood into the Council was secured by a second provision. Three electors were to be appointed, who should choose out of those who had not sat in the council within four years, as many names as the Doge and his smaller council of advisers should determine upon, and the names so chosen were to be submitted to the *quarantia* in the same way as the others. This second provision was so worked as to be favourable to the advancement of certain chosen families. In 1300 the admission of "new men" was expressly forbidden. In 1315 the names of those who were eligible were inscribed in a book for the inspection of the *quarantia* as soon as they reached the age of eighteen years. Finally, in 1319, the three annual electors were abolished, the periodical renewal of the Great Council at Michaelmas was given up, and it was provided that any one who had the right to be inscribed in the *libro d'oro*, the Golden Book as it was called, became, as a matter of course, a member of the Great Council at the age of twenty-five years. Thus, at Venice, a nobleman was said to prove his right to a seat in the council, "*per suos et viginti quinque annos*," that is, by showing that he belonged to a certain privileged family, and that he was five and twenty years old. In this manner the revolution was accomplished, which was called "il serrar del Gran Consiglio," the bolting or locking up of Great Council. It was a gradual movement, and not, as is sometimes declared, a single act.

This change did not take place without considerable opposition. In 1310 there was formed a powerful conspiracy of the popular party, headed by Bajamonte Tiepolo, a member of a family well known for its devotion to the popular cause. This conspiracy was put down with bloodshed, and the heads of it were executed or banished. But it had extended its ramifications through all classes of society. Ten inquisitors of state were nominated, at first for two months, with full powers over persons of every rank, to discover any traces that might exist of the conspiracy. Their power was prolonged from one period of two months to another, till at last, in 1335, it was permanently established by the Great Council and the people, as a regular part of the Venetian constitution. It was this Council of Ten which discovered the conspiracy of the Doge Marino Faliero in 1355, and caused him to be executed. It was this council which in 1432, summoned the great Candotteri leader, Francesco Carmagnola to Venice, subjected him to a secret trial, and caused him to be beheaded with a gag in his mouth, between the two columns on the Piazetta. The members of this council, who were chosen every year, were not allowed to have any family connexion with the Doge, and not more than one might belong to any single house. The Council of Ten gradually came to interfere with every department of state, and got the direction of foreign diplomacy into its hands. In 1559, after the close of this present history, a committee of three were elected from the Council of Ten, and were known as the three Inquisitors of State. With this, the organisation of secrecy in the administration of home and foreign affairs reached its height.

CHAPTER VII.

CASTRUCCIO.

THE period of Italian history which succeeds the death of
Frederick II., is in the greater part of the north of Italy,
the period of the domination of tyrants. Dante says of the
Italy of this epoch,—

> Le terre d' Italia tutte piene
> Son di tiranni, ed un Marcel diventa
> Ogni villan che parteggiando viene.

> The lands of Italy far and wide are full
> Of tyrants, and the veriest peasant lad
> Becomes Marcellus in the strife of parties.

> PURG. vi. 122.

The communes had lost their liberties, and the princely
families who swayed their fortunes, exercised over them
a nearly hereditary domination. Milan was governed
by Matteo Visconti. Its territory extended over the
plain which surrounds the city, and in 1322 was extended as far as Cremona. Mantua was subject to the
family of the Buonaccorsi, who gave place in 1358 to the
Gonzaghi, with whom the Duchy of Mantua remained
till the present century. Passing eastwards, the lordship
of Verona was held by the great family della Scala
or Scaligeri. The head of this house, at the time to
which we have now arrived, was Can Grande della Scala,

the most powerful prince in Lombardy. He became master of the neighbouring city of Verona, having wrested it from the domination of Padua. Ravenna was in the hands of Guido Novello de Polenta, who held it without the disturbance of damaging revolutions. The house of Camino had established itself at Treviso, Feltre, and Belluno, on the ruins of the house of Ezzelino. Ferrara, which had belonged to the house of Este, and had then been a subject of dispute between Venice and the pope, was now restored again to the House of Este. The characteristics of most of these *signori* or tyrants, were the same. They lived for the most part in luxury and splendour, built magnificent churches and palaces, entertained poets, painters, and musicians. The court of Can Grande was especially remarkable in these respects. We are told by a contemporary historian that the numerous distinguished men to whom he offered hospitality had apartments assigned to them according to their condition, and that each had his own servant and his own table. The different suites of chambers were indicated by various devices—triumph for warriors, muses for poets, Mercury for artists, paradise for preachers. During dinner, musicians, buffoons, and conjurors traversed the rooms; the walls were adorned with pictures representing the vicissitudes of fortune; and the prince invited some more favoured among his guests to his own table, especially Guido di Castello di Reggio, who was known by the name of the "Semplice Lombardo," and the poet Dante Alighieri. Among the most distinguished of those who sought refuge at Verona was Uguccione della Faggiuola, who, as already related, had been lord of Pisa and Lucca, and who had now despaired of the imperial cause. It was to him that Dante dedicated the first canto of his poem.

Even under these conditions Italy was not permitted to work out its own salvation, but was largely dependent on the party strifes which agitated Germany. After the death of Henry VII., the succession to the imperial crown was hotly disputed by two claimants : one was Frederick of Austria, second son of the Emperor Albert, grandson of Rudolph of Hapsburg ; the other was Ludwig, Duke of Upper Bavaria. He was supported by John, king of Bohemia, the son of Henry of Luxemburg, and by Henry's brother Baldwin, archbishop and elector of Trêves. To make matters worse, the kingdom of Bohemia was also in dispute. King Ottocar II., who died in 1278, was also Duke of Austria, Styria and Carinthia. His son and successor, Wenzel or Wenceslaus II., died in 1305, leaving a son, Wenceslaus III., and two daughters, Anne and Elizabeth. Anne married Henry of Carinthia, who was king of Bohemia from 1307 to 1310. His sister Elizabeth was wife of Albert I. of Austria, and mother of Albert II., who, by this relationship, laid claims to the kingdom of Bohemia. Elizabeth, the second daughter of Wenceslaus II., married John, the son of Henry of Luxemburg, who was recognized as King of Bohemia from 1310 to 1346. Thus, in supporting the Bavarian claimant to the empire, he was preventing the crown of Bohemia from passing to the house of Austria. Of the claimants, Albert represented the House of Hapsburg, Ludwig the house of Hohenstauffen. Two diets were held for the election of an emperor—one at Rense on the Rhine, which was the regular place of meeting for this purpose, and the other at Sachsenhausen in the neighbourhood of Frankfort. The diet at Rense was attended by five electors—the Archbishops of Trêves and Mainz ; John, who was king and elector of Bohemia; Waldemar, elector of Brandenburg; and

John, Duke of Saxe Lauenburg, who claimed to be elector of Saxony. The other diet was attended by Rudolph, elector palatine, brother of Ludwig of Bavaria. He held the proxy of the archbishop elector of Cologne, who was unable to attend in person. There were also present Rudolf, elector of Saxony, and Henry of Carinthia, who claimed to be king of Bohemia. The diet of Rense elected Ludwig of Bavaria; the diet of Sachsenhausen, Frederick of Austria. The Austrian party found a claimant to dispute the right of Waldemar to the electorate of Brandenburg. Thus on either side there were five electors—two undisputed, three with doubtful claims to the title. Ludwig was proclaimed at Frankfort and crowned at Aix-la-Chapelle, but not by the Archbishop of Cologne, who was the regular celebrant of the ceremony. Frederick was crowned at Bonn by the Archbishop of Cologne. This double election caused great confusion in Italy. The two rivals each sought for recognition of their authority in that country. The Guelphs and Ghibellines, the partizans of the popes and of the tyrants, were each able to make tempting offers, to one side or the other. At length the battle of Mühldorf, fought on September 28, 1321, gave a decisive victory to Ludwig. Frederick was taken prisoner, and the emperor had leisure to turn his attention to Italy. The results of this interference will occupy our attention at a later period.

After the death of Henry VII. the strife of parties seemed for the moment to have found its strongest expression in Genoa. The civil war again broke out in 1314. The families of Doria and Spinola, although both Ghibellines, were again rivals, and of the two Guelph families, the Grimaldi and Fieschi, the Grimaldi attached themselves to the Doria, the Fieschi to the Spinola. Eventually the

Spinola were driven out of the town, and the Doria remained behind as masters. In 1307 the Grimaldi and
the Fieschi made an arrangement to admit the Spinola into
the town if they came without arms; the Doria seeing this
became frightened and left the city. Upon this the old
Guelph party came together and made Carlo de' Fieschi
and Carpano de' Grimaldi captains of the town. When
the Spinola knew of this they were afraid of falling into
the hands of the Guelphs, and also departed. The two
Ghibelline families, finding themselves expatriated, made
peace with each other, and established their headquarters
at Savona. They laid siege to Genoa and invited Marco de'
Visconti, the son of Matteo, to command their army. The
level side was completely invested, and most of the suburbs
were taken. The inhabitants turned for assistance to King
Robert of Naples, who had many possessions in Provence
and Piedmont. The King arrived in person, on July 20,
and the *signoria* of Genoa was shortly afterwards made over
to him for ten years, conjointly with Pope John XXII.,
who had succeeded Clement V. at Avignon in 1316. The
war was carried on by sea and land, not only in the immediate territory of Genoa itself, but in every portion of
their wide dominions. King Frederick of Sicily was dragged
into it during its continuance, as also Castruccio degli
Interminelli, the lord of Lucca. After many vicissitudes of
fortune the struggle ended by the election of Simon Boc-
canegra as Doge. An interesting picture of the time is also
afforded by the career of Castruccio, whose earlier fortunes
have been already related. Tuscany was at this time the chief
stronghold of the Guelph party in Italy. The four towns of
Florence, Siena, Perugia, and Bologna united together in
a compact league, strong enough to make head against

their surrounding enemies. Bologna, although situated on the other side of the Apennines, was always included in this arrangement for mutual defence. On the other hand, Pisa and Arezzo, situated on either side of Florence, were devoted to the Ghibelline cause. Pisa was at this time free, Arezzo was governed by its bishop. The towns of the Romagna were for the most ruled by petty tyrants, and were devoted to Ghibelline interests. Rimini was governed by the Malatesta, Forlì by the Ordelaffi, Faenza by the Manfredi; Ravenna, as has been before mentioned, by Guido da Polenta. Pistoia, Prato, San Miniato, and Volterra were all Guelph, so that the Guelph party was able to hold its own although surrounded by a fringe of powerful Ghibellines. This latter party was now to receive a strong and unexpected accession in the person of Castruccio degli Interminelli.

Castruccio, after he had commanded the army of Lucca for three years, was invested with the *signoria* in 1320. He had already got together a powerful army from all sources, and he soon found an opportunity of making use of it. In 1320 Philip of Valois, son of Charles of Valois, cousin to the king of France, and himself destined to ascend the French throne under the title of Philip VI., was urged by Pope John XXII. to march into Italy to assist the Guelphs and to reduce the Ghibellines. At Novara he was met by the ambassadors of the Visconti, who, partly by presents and partly by cajolery, persuaded him to return without effecting anything. Castruccio, taking advantage of this attack on the Ghibellines, invaded the territory of Florence and captured their forts. He advanced towards Genoa, which was at that time being besieged by the Ghibellines, and took several fortresses belonging to the Guelphs. In the next year the

Florentines secured the assistance of the Marquis Malaspina, lord of the Lunigiana, a territory at the head of the Gulf of Spezzia. By his co-operation, Castruccio was attacked on both sides. In 1322 Castruccio turned his attention to Pistoia, a city lying between Florence and Lucca, and exposed to danger from both places. With the assistance of the Abbate da Pacciana, the Bishop and all the friends of the Florentines were driven out, the signory was given to Pacciana, and Castruccio received a yearly tribute of 4000 gold ducats. At this time Castruccio was so much alarmed at the sudden attack against Count Neri, the tyrant of Pisi, and the murderer of Count Frederick of Urbino, that he built himself a strong palace, furnished with twenty-nine towers, to keep the town in order. In the following year Castruccio advanced against Prato, situated between Pistoia and Florence, which he desired to make tributary in the same manner as Pistoia. The Florentines, however, came to its assistance with a large force, and Castruccio was compelled to retire. The *popolani* in the Florentine army were eager to march straight upon Lucca and to put an end to the authority of the tyrant, but the *grandi* were unwilling to take so strong a step. At this juncture Florence was considerably weakened by the treachery and desertion of a *condottiere* or captain of mercenary troops, Giacomo di Fontanabuona, who passed over to the side of Castruccio. This is perhaps the first instance of the untrustworthiness of hired soldiers which will meet us again and again in the course of this history.

In other respects the condition of Florence at this time was not a very happy one. The *signoria* of King Robert of Naples came to an end in 1321, and it was not renewed. The city was governed by the *gonfaloniere* and the *priors* as before, the ordinances of justice were again put into force, and in 1323 a method was instituted of electing to office by lot. This was a democratic measure, and it admitted many to the government who would not have obtained the position in the ordinary way. The year 1324 was uneventful. In 1325, on May 5, Castruccio obtained possession of Pistoia, sold to him by Filippo de' Tedici for 10,000 gold florins. The Florentines were driven to engage another mercenary leader in the person of Raimondo de Cardona. He took the field with a considerable army and with great energy, and in the months of July and August contrived to get possession of the castles of Coppiano and Montefalcone, and especially of Altopascio, a strong place of great importance. After this first success, Cardona wasted valuable time in which he might have crushed Castruccio, and made money by selling letters of leave to rich soldiers serving under him. Castruccio had during this interval of neglect received large reinforcements from the Visconti of Milan. On September 23 was fought the disastrous battle of Altopascio, in which the Florentines were entirely defeated, the captured castles were retaken, and Castruccio's headquarters were advanced to Signa. On October 2 he established himself in Peretola, only two miles from the walls of Florence; the whole of the fertile plain covered by the luxurious villas of the Florentines was entirely devastated and turned into a desert. The pictures and statues with which they had been filled were sent to adorn the palaces of Lucca. At last the remorseless enemy retired. Signa was fortified, to be a permanent source of annoyance and attack, and on the day of St Martin, Castruccio made a triumphant entry into Lucca. The *caroccio* of Florence was drawn along the streets by oxen, its *martinella* or bell tolling

dolefully as the carriage moved on. Behind the car
marched Raimondo da Cardona and the Florentine captains with candles in their hands. The money which
Castruccio received for the ransom of the captives supplied
the sinews for a continuance of the war.

The battle of Altopascio was not the only blow levelled
at the Guelph cause. On November 15, 1325, the citizens
of Bologna, already hard pressed by the surrounding
Ghibellines, were entirely defeated at the battle of Mon-
teveglio. The Florentines, in their time of need, turned to
their old protector, King Robert of Naples, who had lately
returned from the Papal Court at Avignon, and had accepted
for another period the *signoria* of Genoa. They sent ambassadors to him at Naples. He showed no great readiness to
yield to their request, and demanded as a condition that
either he or his son should be made masters of the town.
They concluded by preferring his son to himself, and on
January 13, 1326, Charles, Duke of Calabria, was made lord
of Florence for ten years. Charles sent before him as his
lieutenant, Walter de Brienne, Duke of Athens, a man who
played an important part in the history of Florence.

The signory of Athens had come into existence in the
beginning of the thirteenth century, in the person of Otto de
la Roche-sur-l'oignon. The same family possessed fiefs at
Argos, Nauplia, and Thebes. The fief was raised to a dukedom by Louis IX. in 1260, and passed through an heiress to
Hugo de Brienne, Count of Lecce. In 1311 the territory of
Athens was overrun by a band of wandering mercenaries,
known at this time by the general name of "Catalans."
Walter II. of Brienne was defeated at the battle of
Cephissus and deposed. These so-called "Catalans" have
a curious history. They had been collected together from

different countries, but principally from Arragon, to defend Sicily against the attack of the Avignon kings. In 1302, in alarm at being disbanded at the approach of peace, they offered themselves to Andronicus Palæologus, Emperor of Constantinople, to assist him in recovering Asia from the Turks. At this time Pope Clement V. was organising a great Latin campaign against the Greek emperor. He had hopes of establishing Charles of Valois at Constantinople in right of his wife, Catherine Courtenay. Frederick of Sicily engaged to contribute assistance, and he thought that he could rely on the fidelity of his Catalans. This made them an object of suspicion to Andronicus. Just at this juncture a very serious war was raging between Genoa and Venice, and in this domestic quarrel Genoa took the side of the Emperor and Venice the side of the Catalans. By the help of Venice the Catalans were enabled to establish themselves in Greece. Having conquered Athens they bestowed the dukedom on Frederick of Sicily, who passed on the title to his heirs.

The Duke of Calabria made his entry into Florence on August 29, 1326, having passed by Siena, and having accepted the signory of that city for five years. The Florentine army, reinforced from the sources we have enumerated, was now of considerable size. The Ghibellines sought to oppose their preparations by still greater efforts. Ludwig of Bavaria, whose career up to the battle of Mühldorf has been narrated above, had made an arrangement with his rival Albert in 1325, by which the imperial dignity should be shared between them, the real power, however, remaining with Ludwig. In February 1327 he was met at Trent by all the most powerful Ghibellines of Italy—Marco Visconti, Obizzo d'Este, and Cane della Scala, as well as the ambas-

sadors of Frederick of Sicily and Castruccio. Ludwig
promised that he would come to Italy to receive the imperial crown, and the Ghibellines engaged in return that
they would pay his expenses. On May 20 the emperor
was crowned with the iron crown of Italy in the church
of Sant' Ambrogio at Milan. As he advanced further south
one of the first duties which fell upon him was to conquer
the loyal city of Pisa. Pisa, which had always been devoted
to the Ghibelline cause, which had been the first to welcome
Henry of Luxemburg, which had provided him with a
refuge in his difficulties and given him a tomb, was now
unwilling to submit herself to Ludwig, for submission to him
meant submission to Castruccio Interminelli. It preferred
independence to consistency. Pisa, however, on this occasion, made but a feeble resistance, as it did not like to
embrace the Guelph cause with too much vigour, and on
October 10, Ludwig, with the help of Castruccio, was able
to enter it as a conqueror. In return for this victory the
emperor made Castruccio Duke of Lucca, Pistoia, Volterra,
and the Lunigiana, and allowed him to quarter the arms of
Bavaria with his own. There was no outbreak of hostility
between the emperor and Charles of Calabria. Ludwig
marched on towards Rome and reached Viterbo on January
2, 1328. The duke, on his part, retired to Aquila. On
January 17 the great ceremony of the coronation took place.
The emperor and the people went in procession from Santa
Maria Maggiore to St Peter's. Castruccio, as Count
Palatine of the Lateran, carried the imperial sword. The
coronation was performed by the bishops of Venice and
Aleria, who had both been excommunicated by Pope John
XXII., a bitter enemy of Ludwig, and by Sciarra Colonna,
the captain of the people. The citizens of Rome conferred

upon Ludwig the dignity of Senator, who transferred it to his faithful friend, Castruccio.

In the midst of these triumphs Castruccio was suddenly recalled to Tuscany by the news of serious disasters. On January 28 Philip of Sanguineto, lieutenant of the Duke of Calabria in Florence, had taken Pistoia by escalade. Castruccio's first act after his return was to sieze Pisa by force, and to make himself master of his resources, when on August 3 he recovered possession of Pistoia. He now stood at the summit of his power. He was Lord, Villani tells us, of Lucca, Pisa, Pistoia, the Lunigiana, of a great part of the eastern Riviera of Genoa, and of more than three hundred castles. But his end was near. He was worn out by continued fatigue and unresting service in war. He was "always covered by his armour, sometimes on foot, sometimes on horseback, to superintend the guards, to excite the labourers, to raise redoubts, to open trenches, to begin everything with his own hands, so that everyone might work in the hottest weather, notwithstanding the violence of the sun." He now fell grievously ill of a continuous fever, and the same disease appeared in his army. He died on September 3, 1328, leaving his son Henry heir to the duchy of Lucca.

CHAPTER VIII.

KING JOHN OF BOHEMIA—MASTINO DELLA SCALA.

By the death of Castruccio Florence was liberated from a great danger. His death was followed by another not less advantageous to the Republic. Charles, Duke of Calabria, Lord of Florence, died on November 9, 1328. He left only two daughters, the eldest of whom, Joanna, has bequeathed an infamous name to posterity. The Florentines were now completely their own masters, and they took the opportunity of constructing a new constitution of a very elaborate character, the nature of which is somewhat difficult to explain. They introduced what was called the *squittinio* or scrutinium, "the scrutiny," the object of which was that no one should hold office except approved Guelphs of popular extraction over thirty years of age. Lists of citizens, endowed with these qualifications, and thus eligible for the office of prior, were made by the following bodies :—first, the six priors and twelve chosen citizens, two from each *sestiere*, or ward, next the nineteen *gonfalonieri delle arti*, or standard-bearers of the guilds, with two chosen citizens from each *arte* or guild, next the *Capitani di parte Guelfa*, or captains of the Guelf party, and their *anziani* or *ancients* in the old English sense of lieutenants; lastly the five heads of the merchants, and the officers of the seven higher arts. The names of eligible citizens, drawn up by these several bodies, were submitted to a board composed in an equally elaborate manner. It consisted of the *Gonfaloniere della Giustizia*, or standard-bearer of justice, who was also called the Captain of the People (1), together with the six *Priori* ($1 + 6 = 7$), the twelve *anziani* ($12 + 7 = 19$), the nineteen *gonfalonieri delle arti* ($19 + 19 = 38$), two consuls from each of the twelve higher guilds ($24 + 38 = 62$), and six men chosen from each of the six *sestiere* by the *Priori* and the *Anziani* ($36 + 62 = 98$). This board of 98 was to vote on the list of names supplied by the bodies we have first enumerated. They voted with black and white beans, the black being favourable, the white unfavourable. Any one who obtained sixty-eight favourable votes had his name written down in a list, the name also being written on a piece of paper which was immediately placed into one of six bags, one for each *sestiere*. These bags were kept under three keys in the convent of the Franciscans, and from them the *priori* and the *Capitano del popolo* were chosen by lot. The bags were filled every two years. The twelve *anziani* and the consuls of the higher guilds were chosen in the same manner. When we read of these elaborate arrangements, whether in Florence or in Venice, or in other Italian towns, we cannot resist the impression that Italian citizens were led quite as much by a sense of quaintness or artistic propriety in making their constitutional arrangements, as by a desire to avert impending dangers, or a sense of political expediency.

At the same time all the existing assemblies were abolished, and two new ones established in their place; first, a *consiglio del popolo*, or council of the people of three hundred members, chosen from Guelphs of popular extraction, and secondly a *consiglio del commune*, or communal council, consisting of two hundred and fifty members, half chosen from the nobles and half from the people. The officers above mentioned held office for four months, with the exception of the priors who only held office for two months. The epoch we have now reached is the culminating point of the Florentine art of the earlier period. Its most distinguished representative is Giotto, sculptor, architect, painter, and friend of Dante. Dante had died at Ravenna in 1321. In 1334 Giotto was appointed architect of the cathedral, Santa Maria del Fiore, and of the walls and fortifications of the city. His greatest creation was the *campanile* or bell-tower of the cathedral, the " headstone of beauty," one of the most perfect works of art ever executed, although it still lacks the golden crown which was intended to complete it. Giotto, who is immortalised in the Divine Comedy, not less than in the numerous paintings and frescoes which he has left to us, died in 1336, before he was able to finish it.

Very different was the fate of Lucca, which had been the capital of Castruccio's sovereignty, and of Pisa so long the rival of Florence. The signory of Pisa had been conferred by Ludwig on his wife the Empress, but it was seized by Castruccio. On his death-bed Castruccio bade his son Francesco occupy the town immediately. He obeyed these but was forced to retire on the return of the Emperor from the South, who entered Pisa on September 21, eighteen days after Castruccio's death. Ludwig then conferred the office on Tarlatino dei Tarlatini of Arezzo. The widow and son of Castruccio, dreading the vengeance of the Emperor for their seizure of Pisa, attempted to establish themselves in Lucca by entering into negotiations with their ancestral enemies the Florentines. Ludwig on hearing of this abolished the duchy of Lucca, which he had created for Castruccio, and restored to the town its freedom on the payment of a large subsidy. The family of Castruccio went into exile at Pontremoli, and the Emperor returned to Pisa. After this Lucca was destined to undergo the most humiliating vicissitudes. A number of Ludwig's Netherlandish troops who could not obtain their arrears of pay from the Emperor, rose in mutiny against him, and encamped on a mountain called Cerruglio di Vicinaja, situated about half way between Pisa and Lucca. Marco Visconti was sent to treat with them, but they detained him as a hostage for the 60,000 gold florins which they declared were owing to them by the Emperor. Ludwig in his turn bade them extort the money from the Visconti, whose representative they had in pledge. In the spring of 1329 a rising took place in Lucca in favour of the Duchini or little Dukes, as Castruccio's children were called. Ludwig, hearing of this, marched upon the town, and appointed as imperial vicar over it Francesco degli Interminelli, the uncle of the Duchini for the consideration of 22,000 florins. On April 11, the Emperor left Pisa and returned to Lombardy. No sooner was his back turned than the Netherlandish mercenaries under the leadership of their captain Marco Visconti, marched from the Cerruglio, and obtained possession of Lucca, with the help of some Genoese mercenaries who had been in Castruccio's pay, and had now passed over to Francesco. Francesco, under compulsion, made over the signory of Lucca to Marco Visconti, and the mercenaries were ready to sell the town to anyone who would pay them for it the arrears of pay which they demanded. They first offered the city to the Florentines, but the negotiations fell through. Florence had in the meantime made a treaty with Pistoia,

on May 24 1329, which was a subject of great rejoicing in
both towns. In June, Count Fazio Donaratico, with the
help of German mercenaries drove the imperial vicar
Tarlatino dei Tarlati out of Pisa, and proclaimed its
independence. He next tried to get possession of Lucca,
being very much afraid lest it should fall into the hands
of the Florentines. Marco Visconti being sent to Florence
to negotiate for the sale of Lucca, contrived to escape to
his native Milan, where he shortly afterwards died. The
Pisans were so anxious to get possession of Lucca that
they paid the 60,000 gold florins before they had secured
the town, consequently, the wily mercenaries kept the
money and refused to open the gates. Pisa was so much
impoverished by this loss that she was obliged to make
peace with Florence in August. Eventually, a purchaser
was found for Lucca, in the person of Gherardo Spinola
of Genoa. He paid the 60,000 florins, and received the
title of *Pacificator et dominus generalis civitatis Lucanæ*.
He governed the city well, and won the affection of its
inhabitants.

At the same time the Florentines did not desist from
their attempts to gain possession of the city which they
had so long coveted. They captured a number of the
surrounding castles, and brought Gherardo Spinola into
such difficulties that he would have been glad to have sold
the town to the Florentines for the sum he had already
paid for it. But the Florentines were again unable to
agree amongst themselves, and the opportunity was allowed
to slip. At last, Spinola made over the signory to John,
king of Bohemia, a new actor who had appeared upon the
scene, to whose fortunes we must now address ourselves.

As has been stated above, John, king of Bohemia, was

the son of the Emperor Henry VII. of Luxemburg. He claimed the crown of Bohemia in right of his wife, Elizabeth of Bohemia, sister of Wenceslaus III., daughter of Wenceslaus II., and grand-daughter of Ottokar II. He found the rough Bohemians difficult to govern, and was obliged to put down rebellions which were not unfrequently headed by his wife. He was devoted to all chivalrous pleasures and pursuits, and preferred to live in his hereditary state of Luxemburg, and to leave the government of Bohemia to the Count of Lippe. John had always been a strong supporter of the Emperor Ludwig of Bavaria. We have seen the ill success which attended this emperor in Tuscany. He did not fare any better in Lombardy. He was strongly opposed by the Visconti, the lords of Milan, and when on the death of the rival Emperor Frederick, his brothers Albert and Otto of Austria prepared to invade Bavaria, Ludwig determined to leave Italy to herself, and crossed the Alps to defend his hereditary states.

At the close of the year 1330, John of Bohemia found himself at Trent in the Tyrol. Here he was approached by ambassadors from Brescia, a Guelphic town, which had done its best to maintain its independence in the midst of powerful Ghibelline neighbours. These envoys offered the signory of their city to John, as to a prince of a noble and chivalrous character, who had nothing to gain for himself, and was likely, if any body, to establish a firm and equitable government, strong enough to keep both parties in order, and sufficiently just to favour neither. Such a deliverer had Dante longed for in vain. John accepted the invitation. He told Mastino della Scala, who had been attacking Brescia, to keep his hand off from a town which was now under protection. On the last day of the year 1330 John made his public entry into Brescia. He recalled the Ghibelline exiles and made peace in the city. The rest of the Lombard cities were now eager to claim a share in these benefits, and to follow the example of Brescia. Bergamo submitted herself on January 12, 1331, Lucca on January 26, Pavia, Vercelli, and Novara followed the same course during the month of February. In March John made a solemn entry into Parma and was invested with the *signoria*. In April Reggio and Modena, also cities of the Emilian road, followed the example of Parma, in August Cremona did the same, and, as we have already seen, Lucca sought, in the name of King John, a protection against the designs of Florence. Perhaps the strongest event of all was when Azzone Visconti, in February 1341, recognised the Bohemian king as lord of Milan, or was content to consider himself as his Vicar. He thought it better to bow like a reed before the storm, with the knowledge that John's success could not be of long duration.

Hitherto everything had gone well. In every town the exiles had been recalled, and ancient feuds reconciled. But in such a storm of conflicting interests it became necessary for John to declare himself. No one could believe in a disinterestedness of which they had no previous experience. Every one was waiting to discover what the king's real design might be, and what self-seeking end was concealed under the specious appearance of self-denying and chivalrous devotion. Some light seemed to be thrown on his intentions by a secret interview which he held with Bertrand du Poiet, the Pope's legate, the ostensible head of the Guelphic party in Italy, who had attempted to form a principality for himself in Bologna. Even before this the citizens had distrusted John because he had appeared to favour the nobles. The Ghibelline nobles were now afraid lest he might be engaged in a conspiracy with the Pope to crush their power. Florence had never given the king her confidence. Even his old friend the Emperor Ludwig now became afraid of him, and King Robert of Sicily naturally became his enemy. John finally threw away all chance of success by summoning his son Charles to Parma and leaving him as his Vicar in Lombardy, whilst he himself crossed the Alps to hold a conference with Pope John XXII. at Avignon. At the news of his departure the great Ghibelline nobles of Lombardy seized the opportunity to shake off the Bohemian influence. The heads of the families of Visconti, della Scala, Gonzaga, and Este, the lords respectively of Milan, Verona, Mantua, and Ferrara, met at Castelfranco on August 6, 1391, and formed a league for mutual protection. This league received the adherence of Florence, and of the King of Naples. It was agreed that the towns which had conferred their signory on John should be divided as spoil among the contracting parties.

At the beginning of 1333 King John re-appeared at Turin, supported with the authority of the pope and the King of France. He vainly attempted to recover the revolted towns, and at length, after making a truce with the party of the League, left Italy with his son Charles in October 1333. The country was again given up to anarchy and disorder. The history which we have just traversed is very remarkable. We see from the readiness with which the towns of Italy surrendered themselves to a prince, who was not their sovereign, who had no claims over them, who was, in a certain sense, a mere adventurer, who had nothing to recommend him but the chivalry and honesty of his character, how eager they were to embrace any expedient which promised them for the moment peace and repose. We know how passionately Dante desired the advent of a deliverer from beyond the Alps. We have seen how monarch after monarch, French and Teuton, Charles of Anjou, Charles of Valois, Henry of Luxemburg, Ludwig of Bavaria, John of Bohemia, were misled, in turn, by the exhausted communities of Italy as the coming saviours.

A letter is extant from Napoleon I. to Murat, ostensibly written at the moment when he was undertaking the command in Spain, in which he wrote, "You will have to do with a new people. It has all the courage, and will have all the enthusiasm which is found in men who have not been exhausted by political passions." The words, if written before the event, were prophetic. The French domination in Spain was assisted by a national rising, which was the beginning of that movement of national liberation, which eventually threw off the Napoleonic yoke. But as it was the exhaustion produced by political passions which threw France and other parts of Europe into the arms of Napoleon, so it was this same exhaustion which made Italy grasp with the energy of despair, at the hope of any deliverance, however illusory. Dante compares Florence to a man in a bed of sickness, who tosses about restlessly from one side to the other, in the hope that each new posture may give repose to his exhausted frame. For Italy there was no repose; the fever had to run its course, until the weakened body yielded its broken will to the bidding of an irresponsible master.

King John before leaving Italy had taken the opportunities of selling a number of his towns to certain of smaller lords. Thus Parma and Lucca were sold to the

Rossi, Reggio to the house of Fogliano, Modena to the Pii, Cremona to the Ponzoni. These petty lords attached themselves, after the departure of King John, to Bertrand du Poiet, the papal legate, who, as we have already seen, had made himself master of Bologna. The Government of Florence had not supported the League, because they had hoped to get some advantage by the spoil of these petty princes, and so when du Poiet was driven out of Bologna by Obizzo d' Este on March 19, "Olive Thursday," which preceded Palm Sunday, 1334, they received him kindly into their city. Embarking at Porto Pisano the legate returned to Avignon with the sense of entire failure. He had not succeeded in putting down the Visconti, nor in preventing the invasion of Ludwig, nor in consolidating the power of the pope in the states of the Church. On the contrary, the Guelph party was more divided than before. John XXII. was now too old to avenge his servant, and died on December 4. The great families of the Lombard plain were now free to extend their conquests on every side. The Visconti of Milan acquired Como, Bellinzona, Vercelli, Cremona, Lodi, Crema, and Piacenza. The traveller in the north of Italy still discerns the wriggling *biscia* or serpent, with a child issuing from its mouth, the cognisance of that house, on many an isolated wall of mouldering masonry. The Gonzaghi of Mantua added Reggio to their dominions, while Modena fell to the house of Este, the lords of Ferrara. It was natural that this powerful confederacy should alarm the jealousy of Venice, and the Florentines were obliged to take the same side by the force of events.

To understand the war which now broke out, we must realise the enormous power of the house of the Scaligeri, lords of Verona. Mastino della Scala was at this time

sovereign over nine cities, which had at one time been
capitals of independent states, Verona, Padua, Vicenza,
Treviso, Brescia, Feltre, Belluno, Parma, and especially
Lucca, of which we have heard so much, and will hear still
more.   Then he enclosed the territory of Venice on either
side.   His revenue amounted to 700,000 florins a year, so
that he was wealthier than any monarch excepting the king
of France.   It is said that twenty-three deposed princes
found a refuge at his court, and it might be supposed with
some reason that he aimed at making himself king of Italy.

The quarrel with Venice, which had long been preparing,
broke out eventually from disputes about the traffic in salt.
The Venetians had a monopoly of this commodity, but
Mastino built fortresses in the mountains and drew a chain
across the Po, in order to bar the passage of the Venetian
traders.   The cause of his quarrel with Florence was his
possession of the city of Lucca.   This town had been sold
by King John of Bohemia to the family of the Rossi,
and by them both towns were again sold to Mastino.   The
Florentines were naturally reluctant to see the authority of
the Veronese potentate interposed between them and Pisa,
between their valley and the sea   Lucca had long been
the prize which they had hoped to obtain for themselves;
for this they had joined the great lords of Lombardy in
their wars against the minor princes.   Mastino had promised to surrender the town to them, but he was too fully
sensible of its value to give it up.   When the Florentines
offered to buy it he doubled his price, and when they
agreed to pay this higher sum he replied that he did not
require the money.   Then they had no alternative but to
join the Venetians in making war against him.   The Venetians committed their force to Pietro di Rossi, one of the

ablest generals of the time, an Achilles in valour, a Galahad in purity of character. As this war went on, this league was joined by all the natural rivals and enemies of the Scaligers—the Visconti of Milan, the Este of Ferrara, the Gonzaghi of Mantua, as well as by Charles and John, sons of John, king of Bohemia. These came together on March 10, 1330, "ad desolationem et ruinam dominorum Alberti et Mastini fratrum della Scala"—for the desolation and ruin of the two brothers Albert and Mastino della Scala. The treaty between Florence and Venice dates from the previous year.

The fortunes of the war turned eventually against Mastino. Padua fell by treachery into the hand of Marsilio da Carrara, who established there a signory for his family. Albert delle Scala, the brother of Martino, who resided at Padua, devoted rather to pleasure than to business, was taken prisoner. Charles of Bohemia obtained possession of Feltre and Belluno, Azzo de' Visconti captured Brescia, Rolando de' Rossi, the elder brother of Pietro, was pressing Lucca, Treviso was besieged, Verona threatened. At length in December 1338 Mastino was forced to yield, and he made a separate peace with Venice, to which the Florentines were compelled to accede. The Florentines did not succeed in obtaining Lucca, which had been their whole object in going to war, but had to content themselves with a few castles in the neighbourhood. The Venetians acquired Treviso and its surrounding districts, Bassano and Castelbaldo. This was the beginning of the land empire of the Venetians, the possession of which exercised such an important influence on their policy, and changed to a great extent the character of their government. The house of Carrara was confirmed in the possession of Padua, Charles and John of Bohemia in that of Belluno and Feltre, while the rest of those who had taken part in the war received their several compensations. The navigation of the Po was thrown open, and Albert della Scala was released from captivity in Venice. The wide dominions of the Scaligers were now reduced to the territory of Verona and Vicenza. However favourable the results of the war might have been to Venice, it was disastrous to the Florentines. It had cost them 600,000 florins, and they had contracted a debt of 450,000 florins more for which they pledged their taxes. Besides this they were in the midst of a commercial crisis. Their great merchants who had lent large sums to Philip of Valois, and to Edward III., found themselves cheated of their money. The Bardi and the Peruzzi became bankrupt. Still they had not given up hopes of obtaining possession of Lucca, and the struggle for its possession led to the events which will now occupy our attention.

CHAPTER IX.

THE DUKE OF ATHENS—JOANNA OF NAPLES—RIENZI.

ALTHOUGH Mastino della Scala had made peace with Florence and Venice, yet a number of his enemies still remained in arms against him, and especially the lords of Milan and Mantua. Opportunity was taken to deprive him of the town of Parma, which was of especial value to him as forming a link between his southern and his northern possessions. It seems strange at first to find the fortunes of two towns so distant as Parma and Lucca, so closely linked together, but we must remember that in the present century, although separated by the chain of the Apennines, they formed a joint duchy for Marie Louise, the widow of Napoleon. Parma was seized by one of the family of Corregio, who were deadly enemies of the Rossi, to whom, together with Lucca, the town had been sold by John of Bohemia. The loss of Verona made the province of Parma valueless, or even burdensome to Mastino, who was therefore glad to sell it to the Florentines for 250,000 florins; this was a very large sum for them to pay, considering the ruinous expense of the war they had just concluded, and the debt which they had contracted in consequence of it. But they were not allowed to take possession of it without opposition. The Pisans could not bear to see the Florentines established in a city which would give them the command of the whole

valley of the Arno, and would seriously threaten their own
independence.   They obtained the assistance of the
Gonzago, the Carraras, the Corregi and other Ghibelline
nobles, and advanced against Lucca on August 22, 1341.
The Florentines collected an army on their side, and
occupied the town with a small number of troops.   The
two hosts were now arrayed face to face.   The Pisans
and their allies besieged each of the three gates, in the
manner of the Seven against Thebes.   At last, after the
chivalrous custom of those days, a battle was arranged
between the two armies, which resembled a huge tournament.   The palisades which had been planted for defence
were pulled up, so that neither side might have an
advantage, and on October 2 the fight took place.   It
resulted in the entire defeat of the Florentines.   Notwithstanding this disaster, they determined to continue the
struggle.   They were able to place another army in the
field, towards the end of March 1342, under the command
of Malatesta of Rimini.   But they were hampered in their
operations by violent floods of the Arno, which prevented
the evolutions of cavalry.   They were forced to retire,
and on July 6, Lucca, the object of so much labour,
and the cause of such terrible losses, yielded herself to
the Pisans.

The Florentines were overwhelmed by discontent and
dismay.   There was serving as lieutenant in the army of
the Florentines, Walter of Brienne, Duke of Athens, who
had on a previous occasion acted in Florence as the representative of the Duke of Calabria.   He was at this time on
his way from Avignon to Naples, and he had been recom-
mended to the Florentines by King Robert of Sicily, as a
man in whom he had entire confidence.   With a fickleness

not unusual in Italian governments of this epoch, they
deposed Malatesta from his command and transferred it to
the Duke of Athens, making him at the same time *Capit-
tano delle Guardia* and *Conservatore del popolo*, and investing him with the *Capitaneriu generale delle guerra* for one
year. At this time there were three parties struggling for
the mastery in Florence, the *popolo grasso* or rich merchants
who held the chief power in their hands, the *grandi* or nobles
who were kept down by the ordinances of justice, and the
popolo minuto or common people, who came at a later time
to be called the *ciompi*, a corruption of *compare* or *compère*,
a French term of good-fellowship, applied strictly to persons
who stand as godfather to the same child. Walter held out
hope to the *grandi* that he would restore their power and
abolish the ordinances of justice. He executed a Medici
and an Altoviti, two of the most important of the rich merchant families; he fined a Rossi and a Rucellai. By this
conduct he won the nobles to his side. The people were
already his supporters, regarding him as likely to rid them
of the tyranny of the *popolo grasso*, and wherever he went
they saluted him with cries of "Viva il signore!" When
Walter thought that the proper time had come, he summoned a general meeting of all the citizens in the great
square of Sante Croce, to deliberate on the condition of
the republic. The priors being afraid that the people
would invest him with the signory by general acclamation,
made an arrangement by which he should continue the
office he then held for another year, that is, to August 1,
1343, on the same conditions as those on which the Duke
of Calabria had held the signory of the city. The next
day, September 8, the people met in the great square before
the Palazzo Pubblico, seized the priors and imprisoned

them, proclaimed Walter signor of Florence for life, drew down the banner of Florence from the tower of the palace, and hoisted the banner of the duke to fly there in its place. The revolution had been effected by the common people, but the *grandi* illuminated and lighted bonfires to celebrate their triumph.

The Duke of Athens lost no time in consolidating his power. He received one after the other the *signoria* of Arezzo, of Pistoia, of Colle di Val d'Elsa, of San Gimignano, and of Volterra. He got together a bodyguard of eight hundred soldiers from the French and Burgundian troops which were scattered throughout Italy, and summoned his family to Italy to share his fortunes. The Florentines had hoped that the Duke of Athens would at least be able to secure to them the possession of Lucca, but in this they were disappointed. On October 14 he made a treaty with Pisa by which Lucca was secured to them for five years, on the condition that the appointment of the *podestà* was left in the hands of the duke, and that the Pisans should pay a yearly tribute to the duke of eight hundred florins in a silver cup. After the expiration of this time Lucca was to be independent, and the exiles were to be recalled. But now a spirit of discontent with the duke's domination began to spread through each class of the population. The *grandi* found that, notwithstanding that the ordinances of justice had been honoured by order of the duke, they were not admitted to any larger share in the government of the state. The *priori* were re-established, and representatives of the lowest guilds were admitted to their college. The morals of the duke and his followers were so dissolute as to form a most severe grievance to all the citizens. It was seen that his principal object was to obtain money for himself, and during the ten months that his domination lasted, he extracted 400,000 florins from the city, 200,000 of which he deposited safely in France and Apulia. He made an offensive and defensive alliance with his brother tyrants of northern Italy, with Mastino della Scala, with the house of Este, and with the lords of Bologna. Florence had never been nearer to losing her liberty, and undergoing the fate of the great cities of the Lombard plains.

The machinations of despotism called into existence many conspiracies to overthrow it, but the Ducal police was so vigilant that the different knots of conspirators knew nothing about each others' operations, and were unable to act in concert. At last, in the summer of 1343, three serious conspiracies were formed, one was headed by the archbishop of Florence, another by two of the Donati family, a third by Antonio degli Adinari. The Duke, when he was informed of these plots against him, summoned assistance from Bologna, and on July 25, invited three hundred of the more important citizens of Florence to the palace intending to make them prisoners. They knew that if they obeyed the summons, death awaited them, so they refused to go, and fortified their houses. The following day the old banners of the guilds were displayed once more, every class in the town rose simultaneously against the Duke, and cries of "Death to the Duke and his followers," "Long live the people," "the State and liberty," sounded in every part of the city. Help was obtained from Vienna and Pisa, and all animosities were forgotten in resistance to the common danger. The Duke made a faint resistance, but before evening he was made a prisoner in his palace. Here he was besieged till August 3, when he surrendered on the condition of safety for himself and his followers. On August 6 he left the city, escorted by the Viennese troops and by a number of citizens. He retired to the castle of Poppi in the Casentino, or upper valley of the Arno, where, with great reluctance, he delivered up the *signoria* which he had so shamefully abused. July 26, the day of St Anne, the anniversary of the delivery of the city, was ever afterwards celebrated as a solemn holiday.

The expulsion of the Duke of Athens was naturally followed by a change in the constitution of the city. The nobles had taken such a patriotic share in this beneficent revolution that it was felt unjust to exclude them any longer from office. The town was now divided into four *quartieri* or quarters instead of six *sestieri*, as the *sestieri* had become unequal in wealth and importance. They were named after the four great churches, Santa Spirito, Santa Croce, Santa Maria Novella, and San Giovanni. Three priors were chosen from each quarter, two from the *popolo grasso*, and one from the nobles, making in all twelve. The *anziani* were raised to the number of eight, one *popolano* and one *grande* from each quarter. The arrangements of the *squittinio* were altered in the same direction. At the same time the *popolo minuto* were only admitted to the lower offices. Probably on this account this arrangement only lasted a very short time. On September 3, less than two months after the expulsion of the Duke of Athens, the people rose once more against the power of the nobles. There was fighting in all the streets, and the bridges between the old city and the oltr' Arno were especial objects of contention. At last the nobles were vanquished, and the *popolo minuto* were admitted to their full share in the offices of the state. A *balia* or assembly was formed in the following manner, consisting of the *gonfaloniere della giustizia*, the eight priors ($1 + 8 = 9$) twelve anziani ($9 + 12 = 21$) the standard-bearers of the sixteen higher guilds ($21 + 16 = 37$) five standard-bearers of the *mercanzia* or lower guilds ($37 + 5 = 42$), two representatives from each of the twenty-one guilds ($42 + 42 = 84$), and twenty-eight artizans from each of the four quarters of the city ($28 + 4 = 112$), making a total number of 196. There were eight priors, three from the *popolo grasso*, three from the *popolo minuto*, and two from the *mediani* or middle class. The *gonfaloniere* was to be chosen from each of these classes in turn. The *grandi* were excluded from office, but as a special favour thirty-five noble families were struck out of the list of nobles, and included in the ranks of the ordinary citizens. This constitution remained unaltered for about fifteen years.

In order to preserve something like a chronological order in this narrative we must now turn our attention to the affairs of Naples and Rome, especially in connection with two very striking personalities, Joanna of Naples and Cola di Rienzi. Charles Duke of Calabria, who died in 1328, fifteen years before his father Robert of Naples, left two daughters, Giovanna and Maria. They were betrothed at a very early age to their two cousins Lewis and Andrew, princes of Hungary. These were the sons of Caroberto or Charles Robert, King of Hungary, who was son of Charles Martel, King of Hungary, elder brother of Robert, King of Naples, both being sons of Charles II., and grandsons of the original Charles of Anjou. Lewis, betrothed to Maria, afterwards became Lewis the Great, King of Hungary, and does not now concern us. Andrew, betrothed to Joanna, was brought to Naples to be educated in 1322, being then

seven years old, his future bride being two years younger.
On January 16, 1343, King Robert died, at the age of
eighty. He had been deeply affected by the death of his
son Charles, and since that event had shown little energy
for affairs. The crown passed to his grand-daughter
Joanna, then sixteen years of age, whilst her husband,
Andrew, a thorough Hungarian in birth and habits of living,
was only eighteen. The court soon became the scene of
the most appalling horrors, and to understand them we must
enter into complicated details of family history. Besides
Charles Martel of Hungary, Robert of Naples had two
brothers, Philip, Prince of Tarentum, and John, Duke of
Durazzo. The second wife of Philip was Catherine of
Valois, daughter of Charles of Valois, and empress of
Constantinople. Philip had died some ten years before,
and Catherine's eldest son was Lewis of Tarentum. This
lady was the evil genius of Joanna; she urged her on to
wicked courses, and did her best to sow dissension between
her husband and herself, in the hope of advancing her own
son Lewis to the succession.

The young Andrew did not like to be in an inferior
position to his wife. He had in his own person some
claims to the throne of Naples, as his grandfather
Charles Martel was elder brother to Robert, and the
male line of Robert was now extinct. He therefore
claimed to be crowned king by the side of his wife, and
he attempted to get the Pope Clement VI. to confirm
his pretensions. In fact Clement acknowledged Andrew
and Joanna as legitimate sovereigns of Sicily in January
1344, and sent Cardinal Emmerich to govern the kingdom.
Joanna did homage to the cardinal in the Church of
Chiara, and confirmed the agreements entered into by the

founder of her line.   Still the adherents of Andrew formed
an Hungarian party in the court, in opposition to the
Neapolitan party.   The Hungarian party was strengthened
by the visit of Queen Elizabeth of Hungary, the mother of
Andrew, and by the marriage of Maria, Joanna's sister,
who had been betrothed to Lewis of Hungary, to Charles
son of John of Durazzo.   The Durazzo princes took the
Hungarian side in the dispute, and the Tarento princes
the Neapolitan.   Andrew fell by his own folly.   He
anticipated the certainty of victory, and he bore in his
shield the device of an axe and a block to intimate the
vengeance which he intended to take upon his enemies.
Catherine of Valois was greatly assisted in her intrigues
against Andrew, by a Florentine, Niccolo Acciajuoli, a man
of about thirty-five years of age, who had come to Naples on
matters of business, but was now devoted to the family of
Tarentum.   Andrew was lured to Aversa by the conspirators
under pretence of a hunting party.   He and Catherine
were sleeping together in the convent of Murrano on the
night of September 18, 1345, when the assassins summoned
him from the room in haste.   He was seized, but extricated
himself, and attempted to return to his bed-chamber for
arms, but the door had been locked behind him.   He
defended himself for a long time and cried for help, but, at
length, a cord was thrown round his neck and he was
strangled and hung from the balcony of the wall over a
garden.   A Hungarian maid, who heard his cries, came just
too late to save him, but she roused the monks of the
convent, who placed the king's body in their church, whence
it was afterwards removed to Naples by the help of Charles
of Durazzo.   The Queen remained quietly in bed, and did
nothing to prevent the murder.   Just a year afterwards she

married her cousin, Lewis of Tarentum. Lewis, king of
Hungary, Andrew's brother, prepared to avenge his fate,
and wrote to Joanna in the language of his country,
"*Johannes, inordinata vita praeterita, ambitiosa continuatio
potestatis regiæ, neglecta vindicta, et excusatio subsecuta
te viri tui necis arguunt consciam et fuisse participem.*"
"Joanna, the disorders of your past life, your ambitious
continuance of the royal authority after marriage, your
slackness in exacting vengeance, and the excuses you have
made for yourself, all prove that you were an accomplice and
a participator in your husband's murder." Towards the end
of 1345 Johanna bare a son, Charles. Lewis recognised it
as the legitimate offspring of his brother, and demanded
that it should be brought up in Hungary. At the same
time he asserted his own claim to the throne of Naples,
and prepared to support it by force of arms. The fortunes
and the issue of his enterprise we must defer for the
present.

The condition of Rome during the absence of the pope
at Avignon had been deplorable. It was torn asunder by
factions, in which the great families of the Colonnas and
the Orsini played the principal part. The people of Rome
were represented by the *Capi Rioni*, the heads of the seven
Rioni regiones, or wards into which the city was divided.
At the head of them stood the prefect, and over both people
and nobles was the Senator of Rome, who was appointed by
the pope. This office was held for a long time by King
Robert of Naples. Pope succeeded pope, but there was no
improvement in the state of things. In 1316, Clement V.
was succeeded by John XXII.; in 1334, John XXII. by
Benedict XII.; in 1342, Clement VI. was elected; and in
1352, Innocent VI. At each election the pope was vainly

asked by his Roman subjects to leave France, and return again to his desolate and widowed city. The historian may wonder that Rome had not before this time proclaimed itself a Republic, and thrown off the yoke of the nobles, of the pope, and of his foreign representatives. At last a man arose who was able to give effect to aspirations of this kind. Niccolò di Lorenzo, generally called Cola di Lorenzo, the son of a tavern keeper and a female water carrier, was one of the deputation sent to Avignon in 1342 to congratulate Clement VI. on his election to the papal throne. Although the poet Petrarch was one of the party, Cola was put forward to speak, and he described the desolation of the city, and the robberies of the Roman nobles in such eloquent and elegant Latin, that Clement was astonished. Clement was struck by the ability of the young man. He appointed him apostolic notary, and ordered him to proclaim a jubilee in 1350, similar to that which Boniface had proclaimed fifty years before. Rienzi had studied as a youth the authors of antiquity, especially those that dwelt on the glories of the Roman republic,—Livy, Seneca, Cicero, and Valerius Maximus. He saw clearly the presence of present evils, but he was less acute in discerning the necessary means of reformation. However, by his enthusiasm and eloquence he got together a number of followers, and made them swear upon the gospels that they would give their help in the establishment of Roman liberty.

On May 30, 1347, he took advantage of the absence of Stefano Colonna from the city, to summon the people to the capital and to make them an address. Raimondo, Bishop of Orvieto, the papal vicar, was at his side. Three banners floated before him, that of Rome signifying liberty, St Paul signifying justice, and St Peter signifying concord and peace. He proclaimed a new constitution, the chief object of which was to secure the people against the tyranny of the nobles. Each *Rione* was to have a guard of twenty-five cavalry and a hundred infantry, the bridges and gates of the town were to be fortified, the nobles were to destroy their castles, public granaries were to be erected, alms collected for the poor, a better justice administered to the people. These ordinances were received with enthusiasm, and Rienzi, as we will now call him, was invested with the title of tribune, and with supreme authority to carry them out. Stefano Colonna hastened back, but was prevented from entering Rome and took refuge at Palestrina. The rest of the nobles were driven out. Rienzi then proceeded to pacify the country, and gradually one by one the nobles came in and took the oath upon the gospels to co-operate in the preservation of the *buono stato*. Rienzi sent ambassadors to the pope at Avignon to inform him of what was being done, and the poet Petrarch strongly supported him. The roads were free from brigands, the Catholic world was invited to the jubilee of 1350. The tribune further sent missions to the towns of Lombardy, of Campania, of Romagna, of Tuscany, to the Doge of Venice, the lords of Milan and Ferrara, the Prince of Naples, the King of Hungary, to the pope and the two rival claimants to the imperial throne, to announce the establishment of order, and to summon them to a general congress at Rome to discuss the affairs of Europe. His messages were generally well received, and thirteen towns sent ambassadors to Rome. But his head was not strong enough to stand such an elevation. He gave himself up to all kinds of extravagances, and assumed the airs and honours of royal state. The readiness with which nearly all the towns and princes of Italy accepted his authority is only another instance of what has been before remarked, the eagerness to clutch at any relief from the weariness of political disappointment. At length the absurdities of the tribune culminated in the ceremony of August 1, when he had himself proclaimed with a wonderful ritual "Candidate of the Holy Ghost." He spent large sums on personal luxuries, and had the arrogance to summon the pope and the rival emperors to his tribunal. He prepared to execute all the refractory nobles, and then solemnly forgave them. These nobles, as soon as they were free, betook themselves to their castles and prepared for war. The Colonna and Orsini, ancestral enemies, were reunited in common opposition to their common enemy. The Colonna were repulsed in a hasty attack on the city; Cola was more elated than ever, and took no pains to follow up the advantage he had gained. The Orsini were pressing upon Rome from the north. At length the legate of Clement VI., Bertrand de Dreux, arrived in Rome and declared against the tribune. Count Pitrino of Altamura, a partizan of King Andrew of Naples, who was living at Rome, took the same side. Rienzi in vain tried to rouse the people to arms. He summoned them to the capital, but his eloquence and tears had no effect. At length he said, "after having governed you for seven months, I am about to lay down my authority." He traversed Rome on horseback as if in triumph, and shut himself up with his wife in the Castle of St Angelo. The barons did not dare to enter Rome until three days had elapsed. Eventually Rienzi escaped into the Neapolitan territory, and Rome returned to its previous condition of anarchy.

CHAPTER X.

THE BLACK DEATH—LEWIS OF HUNGARY—GENOA AND VENICE—MARINO FALIERO.

THE middle of the fourteenth century which we have now reached, marks an epoch of change in the history of Italy. It is the time of the ravages of that terrible plague which was known in England under the name of the "Black Death." All students of English history are familiar with its importance in the economic history of our own country, yet the precise character of the changes which it wrought is still a matter of dispute. Bishop Stubbs says of it, "one thing ascribed to it is that it caused nearly all the social changes which took place in England down to the Reformation—the depopulation of towns, the relaxation of the bonds of moral and social law, the solution of the continuity of national development caused by a sort of disintegration in society generally. Another view would regard it as an example of the social law according to which a period of pestilence and distress results in an expansion of national life and energy, and is followed by an increase, after a certain time, in national prosperity." Perhaps, like the effects of a cold and bracing climate, the results varied with the inherent power of reaction possessed by the individual organism. We have not the means of determining what were the precise effects of this calamity on Italy. We

do not know enough of the economical conditions of the
Peninsula before and after the catastrophe.   But we have
records of the terrible ravages which the disease caused,
and in the dreary annals of the next hundred years we shall
not be wrong in referring the helplessness of the Italian
nation to this cause, more than to any other.   The plague,
supposed to have been brought to Italy from the Levant by
Genoese galleys in 1347, appeared in that year in certain
parts of Tuscany, the Romagna, and Provence.   Checked
by the cold of winter it broke out in the following spring,
and in 1348 desolated the whole of Italy excepting Milan and
Piedmont.   At Florence the plague destroyed three-fifths of
the population, including the celebrated historian Giovanni
Villani ; at Pisa it carried off seven-tenths ; at Siena there
died in four months eighty thousand persons.   The town of
Trapani became entirely deserted ; every one of the inhabitants died.   Genoa lost forty thousand, Naples sixty
thousand, Sicily 930,000 souls.   All Europe was laid waste
excepting the Low Countries, which escaped in some remarkable manner.

We must now proceed to relate the expedition of Lewis
of Hungary into Italy, undertaken to avenge the murder of
his brother Andrew.   Before setting out he attempted to
gain possession of the port of Zara in Dalmatia, with the
intention of using it as a base of operations for conquest
in Apulia.   The people of Zara readily submitted to him,
as he came to them with an army of Hungarians and
Bosnians, but the Venetians offered a vigorous resistance,
and he was compelled to desist from the enterprise.   He did
not, however, give up his design.   He set out from Pesth on
November 3, 1347, and passed by the head of the Adriatic
to Udine.   At Padua he was received by Giacomo da

Carrara ; at Vicenza by Alberto della Scala ; at Verona by Martino ; at Modena by Obizzo d' Este ; at Bologna by Giacomo Pepoli. In the Romagna he was welcomed by the principal lords, the Ordelaffi, the Malatesta, the Polenta, and the Ubaldini. Passing by Urbino and Foligno he reached Aquila on Christmas eve. At Foligno he was met by the papal legate, Cardinal Bertrand, who forbad him to proceed any further, but he replied that he came by the will of God, and paid no further attention. His troops took possession of Sulmona, Venafro, Teano, and San Germano. Lewis of Tarentum assembled an army at Capua, to guard the passage of the Volturno, but he was defeated and Lewis entered Benevento. Johanna assembled the representatives of what remained to her of her dominions, and announced her intention of retiring from the kingdom on January 15, 1341. She set sail with three galleys, and reached Narbonne and afterwards Marseilles. Lewis and Acciajuoli found a refuge in Tuscany.

Charles of Durazzo, who had married the princess Maria, who had been originally betrothed to Lewis, had, on the first news of the King of Hungary's advance, given some support to his sister-in-law Johanna, but he now hastened to Aversa to make his submission to the conqueror. He was accompanied by his brother and by Philip of Tarentum, Lewis's own brother. He was treacherously murdered by Lewis on the very balcony from which Andrew had been hung. There is no reason to believe that Charles was privy to Andrew's death, although it is possible that Lewis believed him guilty, and was also anxious to punish him from having married his betrothed bride. The rest of the princes were seized and sent to Hungary. The fickle Neapolitan mob plundered the palaces of the captured princes, and Frà Moriale himself, who was devoted body and soul to Durazzo took his share in the loot. Maria, the widow of Charles, escaped to Provence with her two daughters. Lewis now made a triumphal entry into Naples, and received the homage of the barons, claiming the kingdom as his own by right of inheritance. In May 1348 he sailed back to Hungary, and shortly afterwards sent Stephen of Transylvania to Italy as his lieutenant. Three months later Johanna and her husband, to whom Clement VI. had given the empty title of King of Jerusalem, returned to Naples. A lingering war went on between Johanna and the Hungarians, conducted chiefly by mercenaries, commanded on either side by German leaders. The general of the king of Hungary was Conrad Wolfart, that of Johanna, Werner von Urslingen, one called in Italian Lupo, or Guilforte, the other Guarnieri. In 1350 the German mercenaries were eventually bought off. Urslingen returned to Germany with his plunder; Wolfart and Fra Moriale remained in the kingdom. Many of their soldiers took service with the different houses of Italy, and went to swell those companies of *condottieri*, which were the pest of that country in the times which immediately succeeded. King Lewis returned to Italy in July 1390. He had with him fifteen thousand Hungarians, eight thousand Germans, and four thousand Lombards, which afterwards were more than doubled. There was some talk of a duel between the two kings, but the conditions could not be arranged. He devoted himself to the siege of Aversa, and not being able to take it could not remain any longer absent from his kingdom. The war came finally to an end in 1352. A treaty was made between Lewis and Johanna, and confirmed by the Pope, the terms of which are somewhat difficult to ascertain.

Apparently Lewis only surrendered his title to Johanna on the condition that she should be declared innocent of the murder of Andrew. Eventually Johanna was declared innocent by the Pope.

We must now direct our attention to the rivalry between Genoa and Venice, which resulted in the triumph of the Queen of the Adriatic. We have already seen how the navy of Pisa was destroyed by Genoa at the battle of Meloria. Genoa and Venice possessed at this time the most important navies in the Mediterranean, and the commerce of the world was principally carried on in the Mediterranean sea. The third Mediterranean power of this age was that of the Catalans, then subject to the kingdom of Arragon. The most important navy in the north of Europe was that of the Hanse towns. The commerce of Venice and Genoa had spread like that of the Greeks and the Phœnicians, into the recesses of the Black Sea, and we find the factories and forts of the two rivals in close proximity. The town of Caffa in the Crimea was founded by the Genoese in the middle of the thirteenth century. They lost it in 1308, and purchased it again from the Tartars ten years afterwards, making it the seat of a missionary bishopric. Tana on the Don was another commercial centre. The Genoese founded a colony here in 1330. It was the centre of an immense trade extending even as far as China. Sinope, on the northern coast of the Black Sea, was another important centre, as also was Trebizond, the seat of an offshoot of the Greek Empire, and the chief port of communication with Armenia. This town was almost entirely in the hands of Venice, there being a very close communication, commercial and ecclesiastical, between Venice and Armenia, of which the Armenian convent of San Lazaro is a relic at the present day.

The two rival powers were naturally strongly represented at Constantinople. The quarter of the Venetians in that city was protected by walls, and their private harbour protected by palisades. On the other hand, the Emperor Michael Palæologus had given to the Genoese in absolute sovereignty the suburb of Pera or Galata, opposite to Constantinople. The town was surrounded by a triple circle of walls, and its magnificence nearly equalled that of Constantinople itself. The Greek Empire was tottering towards its fall, and the Turks were already appearing on the eastern horizon. Andronicus Palæologus III., on his death in 1328, had left a widow, Anne of Savoy, and a son, John V., whom he committed to the care of John Catacuzenus, marshal of the palace. There was a natural rivalry between the guardian and the mother. The Genoese took the side of the empress Anne, and the quarrel was appeased in 1347 by the coronation, on the same day, of the three empresses and the two emperors, Catacuzenus having been elevated to the imperial title. But the peace was of short duration. The Genoese seized the Island of Chios; they also seized and fortified the summit of the hill of Pera, against the wish of the Emperor Catacuzenus. In consequence of these affronts he declared war against them. In the spring of 1349 a hard battle was fought between the Genoese and the Greeks, just off the Prinkipo islands, and in this the Greeks were defeated. The Genoese did not pursue their advantage, but made an honourable but short-lived peace.

Just at this time a war with the Tartars of the Crimea stimulated the Venetians to rebel against the monopoly of

commerce possessed by the Genoese in that peninsula.
They determined to found an emporium at Tana to balance
the rival station at Caffa.   Marco Ruzzini was sent for that
purpose with a force of twenty-five galleys.   On the way he
met with ten galleys commanded by Marco Morosini.   The
united fleets attacked fourteen Genoese galleys in the harbour of Carystus in the Negroponte or Euboea, and captured ten of them.   The Venetians were now joined by two
useful allies, King Peter IV. of Arragon, and John Catacuzenus, Emperor of Constantinople.   In the meantime the
four Genoese galleys which had escaped at Negroponte,
joining with five others which had come from Chios,
attacked Candia, which was a Venetian possession, and
liberated their countrymen who had been conveyed there as
prisoners.   In 1351 Ruzzini was replaced by Niccolò Pisani.
He made a violent but unsuccessful attack on Pera, but was
recalled by the news of a Genoese expedition to the Negroponte.   The Genoese succeeded in enclosing him with a
fleet of sixty-six galleys under Paganino Doria, and he was
compelled to sink his ships and to escape by land.   The
next year witnessed a still more terrible conflict.   A fleet of
thirty galleys under Pancrazio Giustiniani, and of twenty-two
Catalan galleys under Ponce de Santa Paz, under the
supreme command of Niccolò Pisani, attempted to force
the entrance to the Bosphorus on February 13, 1352.   The
battle continued during the whole of a very stormy day and
night, and the loss on both sides was enormous.   The
Venetians, however, were decidedly the greatest sufferers,
and they retired from the contest for a season.   The Genoese
now compelled Catacuzenus to sign a treaty on May 6, 1352,
which gave them the sole right to trade at Constantinople,
and engaged to exclude the Venetians and the Catalans.

The defeat of the Venetians in the Bosphorus was soon repaired in the Mediterranean. Pisani, the Venetian admiral, succeeded in effecting a union with a Catalan fleet of forty galleys. Grimaldi of Genoa came out to meet them with a fleet of fifty-two galleys. The battle took place at Loiera, in the northern part of the Island of Sardinia, on August 28, 1353. The Venetians contrived to conceal their superiority of numbers, a common device both in naval and military warfare in the middle ages, and the Genoese were entirely defeated. Ninety galleys were taken with 3500 prisoners, and 2400 Genoese perished in the fight.

Genoa was at this time suffering severely from famine, and she saw no other sign of safety than to submit herself to the hands of the Visconti family, the Archbishop Giovanni of Milan. The Spinola of the Ghibelline faction, who possessed the passes of the Apennines leading into the Lombard plain, had long been in correspondence with the Visconti. The territory of that house extended from Alessandria on the west to the Lunigiana on the southeast. Giovanni was the patron of all the best culture of his time. He was an intimate friend of the poet Petrarch, and he appointed a committee of six, two theologians, two men of science, and two men of letters, to write a commentary on the Divina Commedia. It was perhaps well for the freedom of Italy that the tyrants of the Lombard plain lived in constant jealousy of each other. The rise of the Visconti, rendered all-powerful by the acquisition of Genoa, roused the Carrara of Padua, the della Scala of Verona, the Este of Ferrara, the Gonzaghi of Mantua, and the Manfredi of Faenza to join Venice against them. They all looked for the assistance of the Emperor Charles

IV. of Bohemia, who was preparing to march into Italy. Giovanni Visconti sent Guglielmo Pallavicini to Genoa as his representative; the representatives of Genoa took the oath of fidelity at Milan in February 1354. This arrangement, however, did not last long. In November 1355 the nobles were driven out and the Doge Simone Boccanera restored.

The Doge Andrea Dandolo died in September 1354. He had governed the republic for twelve years with remarkable wisdom and moderation. He was succeeded by Marino Faliero, who has left a name of sinister omen in the long line of Venetian sovereigns. Faliero was a man of great wealth, and was at this time seventy-six years of age. He heard of his election at Verona, as he was returning from an embassy to the court of Avignon. He entered in triumph on October 15. The first weeks of his dukedom were signalised by disaster. After a vain attempt on the part of the Visconti to make peace, the Genoese braced themselves for a new effort. They placed thirty-three galleys under the command of Paganino Doria; the Venetians met them with thirty-five galleys under Niccolò Pisani. The loss of the town of Parenza, and terror lest the Genoese should attack the capital, had caused the death of Dandolo. Pisano was recalled, but on his way home he put into the harbour of Porto Lungo on the coast of Laconia. Here, almost on the very spot where a crushing blow had been inflicted by the Athenians upon the Spartans in the Peloponnesian war, Doria pursued him, and on November 3 succeeded in bringing on a battle which resulted in the entire defeat of the Venetians. Doria returned in triumph to Genoa, bringing with him the Venetian admiral with all his fleet and 6870 prisoners. The defeat of Grimaldi at Loiera was amply revenged. The result of this battle was, first, a suspension of arms and then a definite peace. The main conditions were that the Genoese and Venetians were to restore each other's prisoners, and the Venetians were not to sail to Rome for three years ; also that no Genoese ship was to pass into the Adriatic, and no Venetian ship to pass between Porto Pisano and Marseilles. As a guarantee for the observance of the conditions, Venice and Genoa were each to deposit a hundred thousand gold florins in Siena, Pisa, Florence, or Perugia. The treaty was dated June 1, 1355.

Before this treaty was concluded a terrible conspiracy had been detected and punished at Venice. The conspiracy of Marino Faliero may, or may not have had a romantic origin. It is certain that its real cause lay in the fundamental character of Venetian institutions. We have seen how the government of the republic came gradually to be confined to a close oligarchy; how the Great Council usurped the power which belonged to the people on one side, and to the Doge on the other ; how the Great Council itself was confined to a comparatively few families ; and how the power of the Great Council was circumscribed by the creation of a political inquisition, in the shape of the Council of Ten. Lord Beaconsfield is believed to have invented the term, "our Venetian constitution," in speaking of the English government, meaning to imply that the parliament or "the chambers" as perhaps he would have called them, have curtailed the authority of the sovereign, and absorbed the political influence of the people, and that the parliament itself had fallen into the hands of certain privileged families, namely, the Whig families of the revolution of 1688. It is not certain what end Faliero had in view. The idea has been generally accepted, founded on the evidence of Matteo Villani, that he desired to establish a popular government. Recent writers have thought it more probable that he wished to establish a despotism similar to those existing in the other towns of Italy. Certain it is that he wished to overthrow the exclusive authority of the nobles. One of his principal accomplices was Bertuccio Isdraeli, a distinguished sailor, and a man of the people. It may be that the recent war against Genoa had given an impulse to democracy, just as at Athens the democratic sailors took a position of greater influence when the fleet had been brought into prominence. On the other hand, the Doge was connected with the most aristocratic families of Venice; the republic was now extending its empire on *terra firma*, and had to fear the rivalry of the tyrants of the Lombard plain, the Este, Gonzaghi, Scaligeri, and Visconti. It might be the most patriotic course in the pressing dangers of the state to consolidate power into a single hand. Both views are indeed reconcileable. We see in the republic of Holland that the people were always ready to support the authority of the stadtholders against the oligarchy of the rich merchants. Faliero might believe that he was acting a patriotic part, and that in shaking off the thraldom of the nobles, he was not only true to the history of his country, but was taking the best course to preserve it from imminent danger. These questions will probably never be settled, for the volume of the archives of the Council of Ten, which is said to have contained the full account of Faliero's crime, has been lost beyond recovery.

However this may be, a rising was planned for April 15, 1355. The signal for action was to be the sound of the great bell of St Mark's, which was never rung except by the express order of the Doge. A cry was to be raised that the fleet of Genoa was before the town ; the nobles were to be cut down as they entered the square of St Mark. Amidst shouts of *Viva il popolo!* Marino Faliero was to be proclaimed *principe*. The plot was revealed the day before that fixed for its execution by one Bertrando of Bergamo, who was not in the conspiracy, but had been ordered to execute some minor portion of the plan. He told what he knew to Niccolò Lioni, one of the Council of Ten, who immediately informed the Doge. There was no suspicion that the Doge himself was concerned in the plot, but Faliero showed very little presence of mind. He disputed some of the evidence, said that he already knew other parts of it, and gradually inspired Lioni with a suspicion which he did not before possess. The conspirators were arrested in their houses, and guards were posted to prevent the ringing of the great bell of Saint Mark. The conspirators, when put to the torture, all accused the Doge of complicity in the scheme, and he did not deny his guilt. The Council of Ten did not dare to try him by themselves, but summoned twenty nobles to act with them, forming a body which was afterwards made permanent under the name of Giunta or Zonta. Faliero was condemned to death, and was executed on April 17, 1345, in the courtyard of the palace. The gates communicating with the square of St Mark were closed for fear of a rising among the people. But immediately after the execution one of the Council of Ten appeared on the balcony of the palace, holding the blood-stained sword which had just done its work. The gates were thrown open, and the people saw the head of the traitor rolling in its blood. In the great hall of the ducal palace, where the portraits of the long line of doges form a cornice

below the roof, there is a single gap.   A black curtain covers
the space where a portrait should be, and on it is written,
"Locus Marini Falieri decapitati pro criminibus."   Such is
the story of the victim whom Byron has immortalised.
Whatever judgment we pass upon his enterprise, its failure
had the effect of riveting more closely on Doge and people
the fetters of a narrow and suspicious oligarchy.   Conspiracy rarely succeeds, and is never justified except by
success.

CHAPTER XI.

THE VISCONTI—CARDINAL ALBORNOZ—DEATH OF RIENZI—
EMPEROR CHARLES IV.

WE must now retrace our steps a little to the year 1350, in which Giovanni Visconti, Archbishop of Milan, had succeeded to the power and possessions of that house. Matteo Visconti, the founder of the greatness of the family, had left four sons, Galeazzo, Lucchino, Giovanni, and Stefano. Galeazzo left a son, Azzone, who was lord of Milan from 1328 to 1339. After Azzone's death, Galeazzo's brothers followed in succession—Lucchino reigning from 1339 to 1349, and Giovanni the Archbishop, from 1349 to 1354. Stefano, the fourth brother, had died in 1329, before the death of Galeazzo. Stefano left three sons — Matteo, Bernabò, and Galeazzo; and amongst them, after the death of the Archbishop, the great inheritance of the Visconti was divided. The Visconti now took the place of the Della Scala, as by far the most powerful of all the houses of the Lombard plain. Giovanni held the lordship of sixteen flourishing Italian towns—Milan, Lodi, Piacenza, Borgo, San Donnino, Parma, Crema, Brescia, Bergamo, Novara, Como, Vercelli, Alba— the town in which Lionel, Duke of Clarence, died— Alessandria, Tortona, Pontremoli, and Asti. Not content with this dominion, he did his best to increase his possessions. Bologna, once the property of the Holy See, was governed at this time by the family of Pepoli, who had been placed in that position by the Guelph party in the town. They were induced to sell Bologna to the Ghibelline archbishop for the sum of two hundred thousand florins, reserving to themselves the possession of certain castles. The Bolognese were indignant at thus being transferred, and they exclaimed in their dialect, "Noi non volemo essere venzii," —"We will not be sold." The pope, Clement VI., threatened the archbishop with excommunication. He also summoned him to Avignon to answer for his offence, but he contrived to escape by an original device. He sent one of his secretaries to Avignon to make preparations for his arrival. The secretary began to hire all the vacant houses in the town and in the neighbourhood, and to provide everything for the provisioning and lodging of his master. The pope began to be alarmed, and inquired what suite the archbishop was intending to bring with him. The secretary replied that he had been ordered to find lodgings for twelve thousand horsemen and six thousand footmen, besides the Milanese noblemen who were to accompany their lord. He had already spent, he said, forty thousand florins in preparation. The pope preferred the room of such a visitor to his company, dispensed with his attendance, and accorded him the investiture of the fief of Bologna for the sum of a hundred thousand florins.

The possession of Bologna naturally brought the archbishop into conflict with the Florentines, who, notwithstanding their internal feuds and dissensions, were the steady and persistent friends of the Guelph cause and of liberty. In modern days the railway from Bologna to Florence, following, as railways generally do, the main lines of ancient

communication, crosses the Apennines by the pass of La
Porretta, and comes down upon Pistoia ; it then runs up the
valley of the Arno, and reaches Florence through the town
of Prato. When the Florentines had driven out the Duke
of Athens after a severe struggle, the cities which had
been subject to them renounced their allegiance to the
mother state, and both Pistoia and Prato ceased to belong
to them. Prato they again acquired by purchasing the rights
which Johanna of Naples was supposed to possess over it
through her father, the Duke of Calabria. Pistoia they
estranged by attempting to seize it by a *coup de main*. The
archbishop, who had made an alliance with the little
Ghibelline lords who surrounded in different directions, now
sent an army to attack Pistoia, under the command of
Giovanni Visconti d'Oleggio. The Florentines had just
time to throw a garrison into the town. Oleggio was unable
to take it, and contented himself with laying siege to the
castle of Scarparia in the Mugello.

After the retreat of Oleggio in the autumn of 1351, the
Florentines formed a close league with the cities of Arezzo,
Perugia, and Siena, thus forming what in modern phrase-
ology might be called a strong quadrilateral for the defence
of Guelphic interests. The allies first applied for assistance
to the Pope, who was the natural defender of the Guelphs,
but Clement VI., as we have seen, had already made his
peace with the archbishop, and confirmed him in the possession of Bologna. They then, in despair, betook themselves
to the Emperor Charles IV., although it was strange that a
Guelphic league should call upon an emperor to defend them
against a Ghibelline confederacy supported by a pope.
Charles IV. was the son of John, king of Bohemia, of whom
we have already heard so much, and therefore the grandson

of the great Emperor Henry VII. of Luxemburg. He had
been elected by a portion of the electors in 1346 by the
influence of Pope Clement VI., who declared Ludwig of
Bavaria incapable of reigning. He was not at first generally
recognised in Europe, and was satirized by the ignoble name
of Pfaffen-Kaiser, the emperor of the priests. His father,
John, was, as we know, killed at the battle of Crécy on
August 26, 1346, upon which Charles became king of
Bohemia. The rival emperor, Ludwig, died on October
11, 1347, and after the anti-papal party had in vain tried
to discover a candidate to represent them, in the person of
Edward III. of England and others, Charles was generally
received as emperor. He is considered to have been a very
good king of Bohemia, but is accused of sacrificing the
general interests of his empire to the special interests of
that particular province. Charles did not at that time
accept the invitation of the Guelphic allies. But the archbishop was not unwilling to make peace, and he was probably incited to take this course by the death of Pope
Clement VI. and the accession of Innocent VI. He therefore concluded the treaty of Sarzana in the spring of 1353,
on the basis of the *status quo*—that is, the mutual restoration
of all conquests. Another reason for making peace lay in
the acquisition of Genoa, which we have already mentioned,
and the consequent embodiment of the Visconti with
Venice.

Three events now claim our attention which are closely
connected with each other—the enterprise of the *condottiere*
chief, Frà Moriale, at the head of his mercenary troops ; the
mission of Cardinal Albornoz to Italy on behalf of the Pope ;
and the return of Cola di Rienzi to Rome. Frà Moriale,
more properly Frà Montreale de Albano, was a Provençal

nobleman by birth, and a Knight of St John of Jerusalem.
He had been, as has been already mentioned, in the service
of Charles of Durazzo, and of Lewis, king of Hungary, and
after his departure had remained in Italy and had got together a company of adventurers who were no better than a
band of organised brigands. His first exploit was undertaken against the Malatesta of Rimini, who were partisans
of Queen Johanna. Malatesta, after vainly invoking the
aid of the Guelph quadrilateral, was obliged to buy him off.
Mercenaries from all parts of Italy joined his standard, and
he also received reinforcements from Germany. The few
allied Guelph cities attempted to oppose him, but he sowed
dissension amongst them, and the people of Perugia were
the first to make peace with him. The Siennese did the
same, and persuaded him to leave the territory unscathed
by the gift of sixteen thousand florins. Pisa and Florence
made a certain resistance, but they soon found it more convenient to follow the example of the other republics. In
July 1354 they made a treaty with him, by which, in consideration of a large payment, they secured immunity against
attack for two years. Frà Moriale led his troops into Lombardy, where they were engaged to help Count Lando, a
German, who was fighting in the service of Venice against
the archbishop Giovanni Visconti. We shall follow the
exploits of Lando before the close of this chapter.

Cardinal Aegidius Albornoz was a connection of the royal
family of Castile. He had been made archbishop of Toledo
in early youth, and had fought valiantly against the Moors.
After the death of Alfonso XI. he betook himself to the
papal court, and was made a cardinal by Clement VI.
Innocent VI. now chose him as the fittest person to rescue
Italy from the condition of misery into which it had fallen,

and to re-establish the authority of the Pope at Rome.
Albornoz was well received by Giovanni Visconti at Milan,
and entered Florence in October 1353. He was accompanied on his journey by Cola di Rienzi, who now reappears
on the scene. We have already narrated how Rienzi escaped
from Rome in December 1347. He first sought refuge in
the Neapolitan territory at the court of King Lewis of
Hungary, but when that monarch suddenly quitted Italy,
the tribune went to Genoa to place himself under the protection of the Emperor Charles IV. The emperor, who
did not inherit the chivalrous spirit of his father John,
delivered up Rienzi to the Pope at Avignon, where he
was imprisoned. The friendship of Petrarch probably
saved him from death, and Innocent VI. thought that he
might be of use as a coadjutor to Cardinal Albornoz in his
mission to Rome. The states of the Church were at this
time occupied by a number of petty tyrants who established
themselves in the different towns, whilst the Colonna and
the Orsini contended for the possession of the capital
itself. The first important duty which fell upon the
cardinal was to crush Giovanni, called il Prefetto di Vico,
who occupied a castle on the slopes of the Monte Cimino,
and was lord of Viterbo, Orvieto, and many other towns.
He engaged in the siege of Viterbo and received the submission of Vico with the approbation of the Roman populace,
who put to death Francesco Buonarotti whom they had
elected tribune in imitation of Rienzi. Albornoz now
despatched Rienzi to Rome, giving him the title of senator.
He entered the city on August 1, 1354, under triumphal
arches. He made an eloquent oration to the people in the
capital, formed his government, made the brethren of Frà
Moriale captains of his troops, announced his elevation to

Florence, and received ambassadors from the surrounding towns. But Rienzi had no soldiers nor money with which to accomplish his difficult task. He was much changed in appearance since the time of his early triumphs. He drank too much and had grown very fat. His face was spotted like a peacock, and his eyes shone with a feverish fire. The Colonna took refuge in Palestrina, the Orsini in Marino, whilst Rienzi was engaged in the siege of Palestrina. Frà Moriale came to Rome, counting on the influence of his two brothers with Rienzi, and thinking the occasion promising for plunder. Rienzi threw him into prison together with his brothers, and he was executed on August 29. Rienzi had at first been received with a certain enthusiasm, and there seemed to be a hope of his being able to restore the papal authority. But his popularity was shattered against the rock which had proved fatal to so many who had attempted to establish their power in Italy. The Italian people were to treat of everything but taxes. Rienzi was obliged to raise the salt tax and to put a new tax upon wine. The consequence of this was that in September 1354, a tumult broke out in the streets of Rome. The people assembled before the Castle of St Angelo, and in the Piazza Colonna. Marching together to the capital, they cried—"*Mora lo traditore Cola di Rienzo! Mora lo traditore ch' ha fatto la gabella.*" "Death to the traitor Rienzi! death to the traitor who has imposed the tax on salt." Rienzi attempted to address the crowd, but the rioters knew too well the power of his eloquence. Stones and arrows were thrown at him as he stood in his senatorial robes with the banner of the people in his hand. The mob set fire to the palace. Rienzi escaped to the upper stories, and there blackened his face, changed his clothes, and attempted to escape.

I

The gold chains which still encircled his arms betrayed his identity. He then boldly avowed who he was. For nearly an hour he stood facing the mob, clad half in the garb of royalty, and half in the rags of a barber's boy. Still all hesitated to lay a hand upon him until Cecio del Vecchio thrust his sword into his belly. His head was then cut off, his body dragged about the streets. On the third day the Colonna had his corpse carried to the *Campo d' Augusto*, where it was burned by Jews on a heap of dry thistles.

Just at this time the Emperor Charles IV. began the expedition into Italy which he had been previously invited to undertake. He had been at first solicited by the towns of the Guelph quadrilateral; he was now approached, with more success, by the confederacy which had formed itself under the supremacy of Venice, to resist the overwhelming power of the Visconti. This league comprised the chief princes of the Lombard plain, the Este of Ferrara, the Gonzaghi of Mantua, the Carrara of Padua, the Della Scala of Verona, always ready to turn against any of their number who threatened a dangerous preponderance. The Florentines refused to join the league, considering themselves bound by the Treaty of Sarzana. Genoa, as has been already stated, was in the possession of the Visconti. Just at this critical moment Giovanni degli Visconti, archbishop of Milan, died, on October 5, 1334. "On Friday evening, October 3, 1334, there appeared on his forehead just above the eyebrow, a little boil or pimple of which he took but little notice; on Saturday evening, the 4th of the same month, he had it cut, and as it was cut, the archbishop fell down dead." Thus says Matteo Villani.

The archbishop's inheritance was divided amongst his

three nephews, Matteo received Bologna, Parma, Bobbio, Piacenza, and Lodi; Bernabò—Bergamo, Brescia, Crema, and Cremona; Galeazzo — Como, Novara, Vercelli, Asti, Alba, Alessandria, and Tortona. Milan and Genoa were held in common by the three brothers. Matteo, who was of an easy-going and quiet temper, took the part of a sleeping partner. Bernabò had charge of military affairs, and Galeazzo of the interior. Matteo died in the following year, 1355, upon which Lodi and Parma were given to Bernabò, Piacenza and Bobbio, to Galeazzo. Bologna although ostensibly belonging to Bernabò, was practically made over to Giovanni da Oleggio who had been sent there by the archbishop. The emperor, who arrived in Italy soon after the archbishop's death, was sumptuously received by the Visconti, although he came at the invitation of the Venetians. He was entertained first in Padua and Mantua by the Carrara and Gonzaghi. A splendid embassy was sent to invite him to Milan, offering him a present of two hundred thousand gold florins. In return for this he endeavoured to make peace between the Visconti and the league, but he only succeeded in concluding a truce. On January 4, 1355, he made his triumphal entry into Milan, and was crowned with the iron crown of Lombardy on January 6 in the church of Sant' Ambrogio. On January 12 he set out for Tuscany, and entered Pisa on January 18. Here he was received with very different feelings. The Pisans greeted him with enthusiasm; they had not forgotten their relations with his grandfather Henry VII. The emperor remained in Pisa for two months. It has been mentioned above that the town of Lucca had been placed under the government of Charles during the expedition of his father, John of Bohemia, into Italy. During this time he had built the castle of Monte Carlo to defend the city against the Florentines. The people of Lucca were now eager to show their attachment, but Charles was afraid of offending Pisa by treating Lucca with too much favour. Indeed he confirmed the authority of Pisa over it.

The cities of the Guelph league, Arezzo, Perugia, Siena, and Florence were doubtful how they should conduct themselves. Perugia determined to act separately, as being a fief of the church and not of the empire. Florence and Siena sent a joint embassy. But whereas the Florentines were careful and guarded in their language, and did nothing which acknowledged the sovereignty of Charles, or which cast a doubt upon their own independence, the Sienese at once admitted their position of dependence to the empire. Florence received the reward of her bold conduct. On payment of one hundred thousand florins she obtained full recognition as a free imperial city, and was relieved from every condemnation which during a number of years had been launched against her by a succession of imperial vicars. Arezzo, terrified by its tyrants the Tarlati, followed, at first, the example of Florence, but at last submitted to the emperor. The smaller towns, such as Pistoia and San Miniato, did the same, and the petty tyrants of the neighbourhood hastened to join his standard.

Passing through Siena, Charles arrived in Rome where, in accordance to his agreement with the pope, he only spent a single night. He was crowned in St Peter's on Easter day, April 5, by the cardinal archbishop of Ostia and by the prefetto di Vico, who had been deprived of his possessions by Cardinal Albornoz. At the end of May, Charles left Italy for Germany. He had failed in all his projects, and the issue of his expedition created in Italy a feeling of contempt for the empire which was never obliterated. Wherever the emperor passed he gave the signal for tumults and disorders which he was unable to appease. When he arrived at Siena, the government of the *Nine*, a close oligarchy of merchants, had been over-thrown, and its place was taken by a popular oligarchy of *twelve*, which was just as tyrannical. On his return, he left his brother the archbishop of Aquileia to command the town, but his back was no sooner turned than his brother was expelled, and the government overthrown. Similarly at Pisa he attempted to appease the factions which tore the town in sunder, but on his return the generals broke out with greater violence and executed Gambacorta who had been one of the first to welcome him into Italy. Lucca, which had hailed him as deliverer, had to condemn him as a destroyer. He slunk back through Lombardy without attendants and without honours, as his brilliant German suite had left him after the coronation at Rome. The Visconti could afford to despise him, and made a great favour of giving him leave to spend a night in their city of Verona. Once more the attempt to bring rest and peace to Italy from beyond the Alps had entirely failed.

The close of the year 1355 was marked by the devasta-tion of the kingdom of Naples by the Great Company, as it was called, an army of mercenaries, commanded by Count Lando, of which the notorious Frà Moriale had been an officer, and also by the successes of Cardinal Albornoz in the Marches. The Great Company, a band of robbers and assassins, ready to do the bidding of any one who would pay them, had marched into the dominions of Queen Johanna to satisfy a private vengeance. They devastated Catalonia, Apulia, and the Terra di Lavoro, while the troops which

Acciajuolo, the marshal of the kingdom, contrived to collect for its defence, being disgusted by want of pay, went to swell the ranks of the Company. The operations of Cardinal Albornoz were directed first against the Malatesta, lords of Rimini, and when they were reduced to submission, against the Ordelaffi lords of Forlì; the neighbouring towns were attacked, Forlì and Faenza were taken. Cesena held out for a long time under Marzia or Cia, the wife of Francesco Ordelaffi, but was at last subdued. In these operations Albornoz had to contend against the forces of the Great Company, which had been driven out of Naples by the exertions of Lewis of Tarentum, and was assisting the petty tyrants of the north to maintain their power. It is unfortunate that the confusion of Italian affairs at this time makes it difficult, or indeed impossible, to find a single thread to guide us through the labyrinth. We are compelled to pass from town to town, and the disorder which is generated in our own minds is only typical of the confusion of the political events which we are seeking to unravel. Chronology compels us to say a few words about Venice and Milan. We left Venice at the death of Marino Faliero, and the peace concluded immediately afterwards with Genoa and Milan. Faliero was succeeded as Doge by Giovanni Gradenigo, who soon found himself at war with the king of Hungary. The Venetians claimed to be the masters of the Adriatic, no ships of war but their own were allowed to enter it; on the other hand, it was understood that any ship of their allies was to be safe from attack while traversing it. Lewis of Hungary, who had long sought a pretext for conquests in Dalmatia, found one by the attack of a Hungarian ship by a Sicilian vessel in Venetian waters. Lewis took several towns of the *terra firma*. Conegliano fell by treachery, Serravalle and Mestre submitted, Spalatro and Zara were lost, Turkish pirates appeared on the coast, Crato rose in insurrection. Peace was eventually made in February 1358. Venice got back her towns in the neighbourhood of Treviso, but the whole of the Dalmatian coast had to be surrendered to the king of Hungary. In the meantime the war against the Visconti had begun again. The members of the old Venetian League, the Este, Gonzaghi, Carrara, and della Scala, joined themselves with the Marquis of Montferrat, a member of the house of Palæologus of Constantinople. The Emperor Charles IV. also assisted them, and Giovanni da Oleggio, lord of Bologna. The League conquered Asti, but a more serious loss to the Milanese was Pavia, which declared itself independent, and could not be taken by Galeazzo Visconti, even with a force of 40,000 soldiers. The League summoned the Great Company to their aid. Milan would have been entirely lost if their enemies had been of one mind. The mercenaries turned their attention to plunder, and the Visconti had time to recover themselves. Some of their enemies fell away from the common standard, others deserted to join the mercenaries, who were in the pay of the Milanese. At last the Visconti won a decisive victory in a pitched battle near Casorata, in which all the captains of the League were taken prisoners, excepting Lando himself. This victory, however, was more than compensated for by the loss of Genoa. Profiting by the disasters of its masters, the city was able to declare its independence, and recalled Simon Boccanera, the former Doge. The war dragged on till 1358. The Visconti had lost Asti, Novara, Como, Pavia, and Genoa, but their adversaries could not depend on the allegiance of their German mercenaries, so that eventually, by the good offices of Feltrino, Gonzaga peace was arranged between the Visconti and the other princes of Lombardy. But the Marquis of Montferrat still kept tight hold of Asti, and Pavia refused to surrender its independence; so against these two powers the war still continued.

CHAPTER XII.

THE MERCENARIES—PERUGIA AND SIENA—FLORENCE AND PISA—URBAN V., CHARLES IV., AND GREGORY XI.

THE period of which we are now treating is one in which an important part was played by the various bodies of mercenary soldiers who, under different names, traversed Italy in all directions, fighting, plundering, betraying, stimulating war for the sake of gain, sparing each other in battle, and carving out thrones and dominions for themselves in the universal confusion. It is to the credit of Florence that she was the first to oppose a bold front to the Great Company, and to check the devastations of that band of robbers. At the same time, her internal condition was far from satisfactory. The city was torn in two by the factions of the Ricci and the Albizzi, and government had got into the hands of young and inexperienced men. The *divieto* or "prohibition" had been established to prevent two persons of the same name from holding certain offices together at the same time. It was a precaution against the undue preponderance of family influence in the administration, but it acted very unequally. The older families had many branches and wide connections, and they found themselves by this rule excluded to a great extent from office. The younger families, on the contrary, were called by a greater variety of names, and therefore related branches were able

to share in the government together.   The tendency of
this was to exclude unjustly the most powerful Guelph
families, and to admit those whose principles were less
certain and less pure.   Also there was a tendency to
exclude a large number of citizens from office, which grew
up in the following manner.   The *capitani di parte Guelfa*
had been instituted in 1269 for the purpose of administering
the property of the exiled Ghibellines.   As this gave them
the disposal of a large sum of money they gradually
acquired very considerable power.   In the beginning of
1352 they got a law passed by which any one who had held
an office should, on being convicted of Ghibellinism, be
punished in any manner the signory might determine, but
with not less than a fine of five hundred silver florins, and
besides this he should be declared incapable of holding
office for life.   The accusation was to be proved by the
testimony of six witnesses, and the judges were to be the
captains of the *parte Guelfa* and the consuls of the arts.
This law was afterwards modified.   Two *popolani* were
added to the *capitani di parte Guelfa*, which previously
consisted only of two representatives of the *grandi*, and two
of the *popolo grasso*, and it was enacted that if by a
majority of two-thirds they should decide that any one was
tainted with Ghibellinism, he was to be warned or *ad-
monished* not to take office, and so to expose himself to the
penalties of the law.   Thus there grew up in the state a
class of *ammoniti*, as they were called, excluded from
public affairs, which were a constant centre of disaffection
and discontent.

About this time war broke out between Perugia and
Siena, two cities of the Guelphic quadilateral.   Perugia,
as has been already mentioned, was a fief of the church

and not of the empire, and by being withdrawn in some degree from the struggles of the time it had become very rich and prosperous. With a natural desire to extend its power, it attempted the reduction of Cortona, an old Etruscan city perched on a precipitous cliff. Cortona placed itself under the protection of Siena. The Florentines declined to assist Cortona, but charged the Perugians to desist from their unjust encroachments. The Sienese took strange measures. In March 1358 they hired a German *condottiere*, named Baumgarten, with twelve thousand men. The Perugians were compelled to raise the siege of Cortona, but they returned to the struggle again with larger forces, and on April 10 defeated the Sienese at Torrita, and took Baumgarten prisoner. The Florentines tried to make peace between these two old allies, but the Sienese were determined to wipe out the disgrace of Torrita. They applied for assistance to the Visconti of Milan, to the Prefetto of Vico, and finally to Count Lando and his Great Company. Lando was now in the Romagna, and he asked permission to pass through the territory of Florence. He was allowed to take a path through the Apennines on condition of entirely avoiding the plain of Tuscany. He retained in custody two Florentine envoys as a guarantee of safety. His intention was to pass through the Val di Lamone to Bibbiena in the Casentino. But his mercenary soldiers were difficult to keep in order. In spite of every precaution they plundered and burned two villages. The peasants determined upon vengeance. The mercenary army had to pass through a narrow gorge called *Biforco* or *le Scalette*. The slopes of the hills were occupied by mountaineers. The vanguard, in which were the two Florentine envoys, was allowed to pass without hindrance;

but Lando, with the main body, found himself stopped.
At a given signal an avalanche of rock was let loose from
the upper slopes. The horses were terrified and carried
down into the torrents; Lando was wounded in the head.
At this moment Count Burckhardt with the rear-guard
entered the pass, when a falling rock carried both horse
and rider into the abyss below. The Great Company was
cut to pieces. Lando was taken prisoner, but was released
on payment of a ransom. In the meantime the vanguard
had fortified itself in the Castle of Dicomano in the Val di
Sieve. The Florentines went to attack it, but the envoys,
finding their lives in danger, instead of sacrificing themselves for the good of their country, helped to secure the
retreat of the mercenaries to Tivoli in the Romagna.
Thus an opportunity was lost of ridding themselves of this
pest, and the Great Company cherished an undying hatred
against the Florentines. Soon after this peace was made
between Perugia and Sienna on equitable terms.

Cardinal Albornoz, who had been recalled to Avignon,
returned to Italy at the close of 1358. In the beginning
of the following year he signed a treaty with the Great
Company, which provided that it should not attack the
state of the Church or the territory of Florence, on the
payment of 45,000 florins by the one, and 80,000 by the
other. The Florentines repudiated this arrangement with
the utmost indignation. They were not sunk so low as to
bargain for their safety with a band of brigands. It is
greatly to the credit of Florence that she was the first to
oppose a manly resistance to this extortion, and to re-
nounce a system of cowardly temporizing which had proved
the destruction of the Roman empire. Lando, reinforced
by the troops of Baumgarten, and by nearly all the foreign

adventurers who were then in Italy, stronger in numbers than ever, was now invited to take service with the Marquis of Montferrat against the Visconti. He was at this time in the territory of Perugia, which had granted him a free passage. Sienna and Pisa had done the same, and Lando hoped to terrify the government of Florence. The Florentines, however, strengthened by a number of allies, who seized an opportunity of declaring against a common scourge, placed Pandolfo Malatesta at their head, and determined to defend their frontiers. The company passed from the territory of Siena to that of Pisa, and then to that of Lucca, always skirting the boundaries of Florence. At last the two armies came face to face in July 1359 near Montecatini, between Pistoia and Pescia. Lando challenged Pandolfo to battle, sending him a glove stained with blood. The challenge was willingly accepted, but the German was afraid to risk an engagement. He set fire to his camp, and marched in haste to Genoa. Malatesta returned to Florence in triumph. The Florentines sent a force of a thousand men to Bernabò Visconti, to help him against the mercenaries, but Lando soon left the service of Montferrat for that of Bernabò himself, so that the Florentines and the Germans found themselves fighting on the same side. This accession to the power of the Visconti enabled them to reduce Pavia.

If we followed the strict chronological order of events, we should now give an account of the contention between the Visconti and the pope, which occupied the years 1260 and 1261, but it will probably be more convenient to defer this for the present, and to pass on to the war between Florence and Pisa, which broke out in 1362. The quarrel had began in 1356 about a question of trade. Florence

was now, next to Venice, the greatest commercial city of
Italy.   The natural road for its traffic was through Pisa,
and this traffic was a source of wealth to both communities.   The Florentines had always enjoyed the right of
free entry to the port of Pisa, but in June 1356 the Pisans
imposed a pirate tax on the ground of the expense of keep-
ing down the pirates.   This the Florentines resisted, and in
November they broke off their commercial relations with
Pisa, and determined that in future their commerce should
pass through the harbour of Talamone in Maremma, which
belonged to the Sienese.   Talamone is familiar to students
of the "Divina Commedia" as a place where the people
of Siena had spent a great deal of money without result.
The modern port of Florence—Livorno or Leghorn—owes
its formation to the dukes of the house of Medici.   This
change was a terrible loss to Pisa.   Not only did the
Florentines leave the city, but also the merchants of many
nations whom the Florentines had attracted thither.   The
Pisans tried to prevent ships from sailing to Talamone by
force, but in the end they were obliged to succumb.   This
attempt to force trade out of its natural channel brought
advantage to nobody.   Revolutions broke out at Pisa,
Florence, and Perugia, and added to the universal confusion
and distress.   In 1361 the Florentines became masters of
Volterra, a strong hill town, which the Pisans had always
coveted for themselves.   At length their growing discontent
burst into a flame and war was declared between the two
cities.   Success everywhere attended the Florentines.   They
not only pressed the Pisans by land, but with the help of
the Genoese and Neapolitans attacked them by sea.   Since
the defeat of Meloria the maritime power of the Pisans had
almost ceased to exist, so that they could offer little or no

resistance. The Florentines captured the island of Giglio in the Tuscan Archipelago: they even attacked the very port of Pisa, and took away the iron chains which defended it. These chains long hung over the gate of the Baptistery at Florence until they were restored when both towns became part of a united Italy. The Pisans in despair turned for help to Bernabò Visconti of Milan, himself hard pressed by a crowd of enemies. He sent to their assistance the White or English Company of mercenaries, of whose fortunes we must now give some account. This company was now commanded by a German, Albert Sterz. They were called the English Company, either because the company was largely composed of Englishmen, or because they had been in the pay of Edward III. in France, or because they had adopted the English methods of discipline and accoutrement. The south of France was at this time almost in as bad a condition as Italy. The soldiers set free by the peace of Bretigny, in 1360, were ravaging the country in all directions. The White Company had passed into Italy in 1360 to avoid the plague which was then raging in Provence, and the Marquis of Montferrat was very glad of its assistance to help him against the Visconti. With the usual infidelity of their kind the company passed over to the side of the Visconti, against whom it was engaged to fight. Bernabò was soon tired of these troublesome allies, and, by sending them to assist the Pisans, he rid himself of a disagreeable burden, and was able to defend his friends at a cheap rate.

The English Company arrived at Pisa on July 18, 1363. It consisted of 2500 horsemen and 2000 foot. Filippo Villani informs us that their cavalry was reckoned by *lances*, each lance consisting of three horsemen bound together by strict ties of association. They used their horses to transport them to the place of conflict, but they usually fought on foot. They were covered with impenetrable armour; they wore a sword and a dagger at their side; two men supported the huge lances as they advanced in seried phalanx with loud cries. Each horseman was attended by one or two pages, whose business it was to polish their master's armour until it shone like a mirror. This was the first time that horsemen had been seen in Italy to fight on foot. They cared nothing for the cold of winter, and did not go into winter quarters. For the assault of walls they carried with them short ladders of not more than three rungs each, which could be securely fastened together. In this way they could reach the summit of the highest wall, whilst the ladder never over-topped the parapet so as to be thrown down into the ditch. In the spring of 1364 the Visconti made peace with their enemies, as we shall see later on, and Galeazzo was able to send to the Pisans the German Company of Baumgarten, consisting of three thousand cuirassiers or *barbuti*, so that the Pisans had a larger army at their disposal than any prince in Italy had ever had before. They now hoped to make an advantageous peace with the Florentines, but they in their turn called in the *della Stella* or Star Company of mercenaries from Provence. This company, however, being bribed by the Visconti, never arrived.

The Pisans gave the command of their troops to a famous Englishman, called in the Italian histories Acuto or Aguto, but as we are also told that his name signified *Falcone in bosco*, or "Hawk in the wood," we may infer that his name was John Hawkwood. He was born at Sible Hedingham, in Essex, where the tower of the church built by him still

shows the emblem of a hawk in the wood, and a hospital
endowed by his will, in order to atone for any sins he may
have committed in his eventful life, still exists. His tomb
is also to be seen in Sible Hedingham Church enriched by
armorial bearings. He had gained a considerable reputation in the French wars, and had a good reputation for
honesty, although Filippo Villani says of him that he was a
great master of war, but, like most of his trade, as cunning
as a fox. Also Graziani, another Florentine chronicler, says
of him, "he endured under arms longer than any one ever
endured—for he endured sixty years; and he well knew
how to manage that there should be little peace in Italy in
his time, and every land was, as it were, tributary to him,
and woe to those men and people who trust too much to
men of that stamp; for men, and communes, and all cities,
live and increase by peace, but these men live and increase
by war, which is the undoing of cities, for they fight and
become of naught. In them is neither love nor faith."
He spent the greater part of his life in the service of Florence, and the Florentines after his death painted his effigy
on horseback on the walls of our Lady of the Flower.
Under the command of Hawkwood, who had with him a
considerable number of English soldiers, the two companies
marched up to the walls of Florence, and ravaged its
territory, and even danced round their watch-fires on the
top of the hill of Fiesole, so that they could be seen by the
whole city. After this, Hawkwood devastated the territory
of Arezzo, Cortona, and Sienna, and returned to Pisa by
way of the Val d'Elsa. The Florentines succeeded in cor-
rupting the greater part of these mercenaries, so that they
deserted the service of Pisa, except John Hawkwood, who
remained with twelve hundred Englishmen. He was beaten

K

by the Florentines in a battle near Cascina, in the neighbourhood of Pisa.   The Pisans now changed their government, electing Giovanni d'Agnello, one of their citizens, as
Doge. He was supported by the party of the Raspante, and
by Bernabò Visconti, and he had secured the adhesion of
Hawkwood by a large sum of money.   He was inaugurated on
August 13, 1364, and a fortnight later peace was concluded
between Florence and Pisa by the good office of Pope
Urban V., the successor of Innocent VI.   The Florentines
were restored to all their ancient privileges in the port of
Pisa, the castle of Pietrabuona was given up to them, and
the Pisans agreed to pay the Florentines a hundred
thousand gold florins in ten years—ten thousand each
year, in a golden cup, on the eve of the feast of St. John.

The events which next engage our attention are the tem-
porary return of Pope Urban V. to Rome, and the second
expedition of the Emperor Charles IV. into Italy.   Innocent
VI. had died on September 12, 1362.   His successor was
the sixth pope who had reigned at Avignon since Clement
V. transported the see to France in 1305.   The pope had
bought the sovereignty of Avignon from queen Johanna of
Naples, and it continued with the county of Venaissin as
part of the papal possessions till it was incorporated with
France at the beginning of the French Revolution.   It is
not necessary to dwell on the corruption of the papal court,
or the contempt with which it was treated by Italians.   The
long war between the pope and the Visconti, and the
frequent excommunications launched against the family, did
not prevent them from holding the supremacy of north
Italy, and contracting alliances with the noblest families of
Europe.   But Avignon had ceased to be a safe residence.
The conclusion of the peace of Bretigny had left the

country a prey to hordes of mercenaries; the Jacquerie, the rising amongst the peasantry, also contributed to render it insecure. Urban made a virtue of necessity, and in 1365 arranged with Charles IV. his return to the Holy City. At the same time higher motives were not altogether absent. Italy was now devastated by four companies of mercenaries —the German Company of Baumgarten, the English Company of Hawkwood, the Company of the Star, which the Florentines had invited from Provence, and the Company of St George which one of the Visconti had taken into his pay. The pope formed the idea of liberating Italy from this scourge by turning all the mercenaries against the Turks, whose advance was becoming formidable. Urban wished to hold a congress at Bologna to concert measures for the execution of this plan. We find St Catherine of Siena, one of the most interesting personalities of the middle ages, strongly in favour of this crusade. She wrote to John Hawkwood (perhaps in 1360), "O dearest and sweetest brother in Christ Jesus, it would be a great thing if you could turn your attention a little towards yourself, and consider what troubles and fatigues you have endured in the service and pay of the devil. Now, my soul desires that you should take the pay and the cross of Christ crucified, together with all your followers and companions, so that you may be a company of Christ to go against the infidel dogs who spurn our holy place where our first great truth reposed and endured death and pains for us." It is some credit to Hawkwood that St Catherine should have written to him thus; indeed she implies in the letter that he had already promised to undertake the enterprise. St Catherine Bernicosa was born at Siena in 1347. She entered the Order of the female Dominicans in 1362, and lived a retired life of prayer and meditation till 1368, when she began to take an interest in public affairs. She died at Siena in 1380, in the odour of sanctity. Her memoirs were written by her confessor, Fra Raimondo of Capua. The poet Petrarch addressed the pope in language not less eloquent than that of St Catherine, urging him to quit Avignon, which was the seat of every vice and iniquity, and to betake himself to Rome, where he would find himself in the company of Peter, of Paul, of Stefano, of Lorenzo, of Sylvester, of Gregory, of Jerome, of Agnes, of Cecilia, and of many thousands and thousands of saints who confessed the faith of Christ, and consequently laid down their life for it.

The pope and the emperor had engaged to meet together in Italy in May 1367, but the emperor found himself obliged to put off his journey for a year. The pope leaving Avignon on April 30, 1369, embarked at Marseilles on vessels furnished by Queen Johanna, Venice, and Pisa, and after a few days' sojourn at Genoa landed at Corneto on June 4, not far from the port of Civita Vecchia, which was then in the hands of Francesco da Vico. Here he was received by Cardinal Albornoz, who was able to assure him that during the fourteen years' tenure of his office as legate, he had reduced the whole of the territory of St Peter to obedience. On his arrival in Italy Albornoz had found only two castles which acknowledged the authority of the pope—Montefiascone and Montefalco; now the pope was obeyed by all the towns of Ravenna, of the Marches, of Umbria, and of the old patrimony. The cardinal presented the pope with a waggon full of the keys of towns and castles. Now just when his work was completed he died on August 24, 1367. His last act was to organise a new league against the Visconti, consisting of the emperor, the pope, the king of Hungary, the lords of Padua, Ferrara, and Mantua, and, strange to say, of Johanna, Queen of Naples. Albornoz was also a great lawgiver. The Egidian Constitutions promulgated by him in a parliament of the Marches in 1357 were recognised by Sixtus IV., and were current in the States of the Church till 1816.

The Emperor Charles IV. arrived at Conegliano in May 1368, and reached Padua on the seventeenth of that month. He was accompanied by a large army, but he does not appear in this second journey to have improved the bad reputation which he left by his first expedition. His first exploit was to make peace with the Visconti, whom all Italy and even Europe was eager to attack. Lucca, as we know, had always felt an affection for him. It was at this time subject, governed, as we have said above, by the Doge Agnello. Agnello, in return for recognition, surrendered Lucca to Charles, and the Emperor committed it to Marckwald, Bishop of Augsburg, and patriarch of Aquileia. Agnello was accidentally wounded at Lucca, and the Pisans took the opportunity of deposing him, crying "Viva lo imperadore et muoia lo dogio." At Siena Charles found new troubles. On Charles's previous visit the oligarchy of the Nine had been supplanted by a new democratic oligarchy of Twelve. The Nine had now risen against the Twelve, and were anxious to establish a government in which the *grandi* should have the largest share. The emperor offered to make peace, and effected a compromise which was for a time successful. Having offended the pope by the peace he had made with the Visconti, he now attempted to ingratiate himself with him. He arrived at Rome before Urban V. reached it, met him at the Porta Collina on

October 21, and led his horse by the bridle to the palace
of the Vatican. On November 1, Urban crowned the
Empress Elizabeth in St Peter's. This complaisance only
served to lower him in the eyes of the Romans. On his
return to Siena he was attacked by the parties whom he
had endeavoured to reconcile: was shut up in a palace
with nothing to eat, and was reduced to such a state of
misery and terror, that he granted everything he was asked.
Escaping from Siena with his bare life he was afraid to
enter Pisa, lest a worse fate should befall him, the town
being torn asunder by factions; he therefore went straight
to the friendly city of Lucca, which he restored to its
independence on the payment of 200,000 florins. Thus
Lucca regained in April 1370 the freedom which she had
lost in June 14, 1314, by submitting to Uguccione della
Faggiuola. Charles, on his way back to Germany, thought
of nothing but amassing money. He exacted it on one
pretext or another from Pisa, from Florence, and from
other sources, and he used this treasure to beautify his
capital of Prague, especially in building the bridge which
still exists across the Moldau.

In the meantime Pope Urban V. added to the lustre of
a victory over the Emperor of the West, the submission
of the Emperor of the East. John Palæologus came to
Rome in 1369 to implore the aid of Christendom against
the Turks, who under Amurath were threatening Constantinople. He recognised the pope's supremacy, abjured his
heresies, and accepted the doctrines of the catholic faith.
The document, drawn up in Greek and Latin, was sent to
all catholic churches. He too held the pope's bridle as he
rode in procession to the Vatican. He obtained in return
empty bulls and promises, but was arrested on his return

at Venice for debt.   It is a strange episode in the history of
the widowed city that she should have seen in two years the
two great potentates of the world in submission to the spiritual
power, whose yoke she herself had so long rejected.   Urban
had the further success of reducing Perugia to obedience,
and rousing Florence against the Visconti.   The war
between France and England, which had for a time been
suspended by the peace of Bretigny, now broke out again.
Urban yielded to the persuasions of the French cardinals,
who persuaded him that his presence was required in the
north in order to reconcile the combatants.   He embarked
at Corneto on September 5, 1370, and on the 24th of the
same month was received with exultation at Avignon.
He never, however, recovered from the fatigue of the
journey, and died on December 19.

The papal see was filled, before the close of the year, by
the election of Pierre Roger de Beaufort, who took the name
of Gregory XI.   He asked St Catherine of Siena to pray
for him and for the church—a demand which gave her
great pleasure and hope for the future.   The new pope
shortly found himself in violent conflict with the Visconti,
and the war began to go against them, owing to the defec-
tion of John Hawkwood, who being dismissed by the
tyrant of Milan, took refuge with the legate of the pope.
A truce was concluded at Bologna, June 4, 1375, after
which Hawkwood left the service of the church and marched
his company into Tuscany.   This, with other reasons, produced a violent change in the political relations of Florence.
The provinces of Bologna and Perugia were governed for
the pope by French legates, who exhibited the lust and
avarice which have so often tended to rouse Italians to
rebel against French domination.   There were disputes

about corn, and soreness about the tardy assistance given
to the pope in his war against the Visconti. St Catherine
in vain tried to maintain peace between Florence and the
Holy See.   Hawkwood was bought off by a large payment
of money, and new officers were appointed at Florence,
called the *otto di guerra*, or the " eight of war."   The
Florentines determined to strengthen the rebellion which
had broken out against the papal government, and to seek
the alliance of the Visconti.   They chose "libertà" as the
device for their standard.   There was a general rising in
all the states of the church ; eighty towns threw off their
allegiance in three days.   The pope replied by placing
Florence under an interdict, and confiscated the property
of Florentine merchants—a sentence which was taken full
advantage of by the creditors of Florence in France and
England.   The Florentines continued their struggle with
such eager enthusiasm that the *otto di guerra* were known by
the name of the *otto santi* the " eight saints."   Bologna
threw off the papal yoke, and the banner of liberty was sent
to Rome.   St Catherine did all she could to bring about
peace.   She went to Florence and persuaded the government to send ambassadors to Avignon.   She then repaired
thither herself, and was well received by the pope.   Although
she failed in reconciling the combatants, she succeeded in
persuading Gregory XI. that the one hope of recovering
the dominions of the church lay in his personal presence in
Italy.   The pope left Avignon on September 13, 1376,
embarked at Marseilles, and on January 17, 1377, landed
at the Basilica of St Paul.   The Babylonish captivity was at
an end.

CHAPTER XIII.

THE VISCONTI—THE GREAT SCHISM—REVOLUTION OF THE CIOMPI AT FLORENCE.

IN describing the events above narrated we have omitted the special history of the Visconti family, lords of Milan; to this we must now give our attention. We have seen how the Archbishop of Milan, Giovanni, was succeeded by his three nephews, Matteo, Galeazzo, and Bernabò; how Matteo died, and his possessions were divided amongst his brothers. For the twenty years during which they were the principal lords of the Lombard plain, they maintained an almost unceasing war with the tyrants of Verona, Mantua, Padua, and, what is more important, with the pope and his legates. Neither the strength of their rivals, nor the violence of ecclesiastical censurers, were sufficient to over-throw them, and their most brilliant period was yet to come. The year 1306 found them at war with the league, headed by the Marquis of Montferrat, and supported by the mer-cenaries of Lando. The victory of Casorate gave a decisive victory to the Visconti. The loss of Genoa turned the scale in favour of their enemies, and their position was rendered worse by the ability of the pope's legate, Cardinal Albornoz. At last peace was made in 1358; the Visconti surrendered Asti and Novi to Montferrat, and they were unable to recover Pavia. This town, however, came into the

possession of Galeazzo in the following year. The war with
the pope still continued, the chief struggle being for the
possession of Bologna. This had been occupied, as we
have seen above, by Giovanni d' Oleggio, a relation of the
Visconti. Oleggio was persuaded to exchange this for the
Marquisate of Fermo, and took possession of Bologna for the
pope. In 1360 the house of Visconti received additional
splendour by an alliance with the royal house of France.
Gian Galeazzo, son of Galeazzo, married Isabelle of Valois,
daughter of King John. His wife brought to him, as part of
her dowry, the county of Vertus in Champagne, so that he
was called Conte di Virtù (Comes Virtutum), half in
honour and half in jest. In the following year Bernabò
made peace with the pope, and surrendered all hope of
recovering Bologna. The struggle with the Marquis of
Montferrat for Pavia still continued, and the Marquis, as
has been before mentioned, invited the White Company of
English mercenaries from Provence to assist him. This
proved as great a scourge to the west of Lombardy as the
Hungarians of King Lewis had shown themselves to the
east. They also brought the plague with them, and 79,000
inhabitants of Milan died of it. A story found in the
chronicles of this period throws light on the relations between the Visconti and the pope. In 1361 envoys were
sent to Bernabò from Innocent VI. with a papal letter.
Bernabò met the messengers at a bridge over the river
Lambro. Bernabò took the letter and read it, and with a
stern countenance asked them whether they would rather
eat or drink. They looked at the rushing river, and said
that they would prefer to eat, upon which Bernabò made
them eat up the whole brief, parchment, silk, and leaden
seal. To wash out this insult Innocent VI., in 1312, got

together another league, comprising the Carrara, della Scala, and Gonzaghi.   The contest raged chiefly around Brescia.

Pope Urban V., who succeeded to the papal see in the following year, was one of the ambassadors who had been made to eat the brief, and after a fruitless attempt at peace he launched a fresh ban against Bernabò in March 1363. The Visconti struggled stubbornly against tremendous odds, and after several defeats ended by concluding peace on more favourable terms than they could have expected, by the mediation of the kings of France and Hungary.   The treaty was published on March 3, 1364.   Bernabò resigned all claim whatever to Bologna, the rest of his relations to the league remaining in *statu quo*.   Galeazzo, on his part, gave up Asti to Montferrat, but retained Pavia, Alba, and Novara.

The cessation of external war gave the Visconti leisure to turn their attention to their private affairs.   It is almost impossible to imagine the tyranny with which Milan was governed.   A decree of Galeazzo's is extant, in which he gave directions for the torturing and killing of his enemies. The process is to last exactly forty-one days.   For the first fourteen days they are to be tortured with stripes and nauseous drinks—every alternate day being one of rest in order to prolong the agony ; on the fifteenth day the soles of their feet are to be skinned, and they are to be made to walk on peas ; on the nineteenth day they are to ride the wooden horse ; on the twenty-third day one eye is to be taken out ; on the twenty-fifth day the nose is to be cut off ; on the thirty-first day one foot is to be cut off ; on the thirty-third, the other.   Tortures still more disgusting and revolting follow, till at last, on the forty-first day, they are broken on the wheel.   Bernabò was especially fond of boar-hunting, and kept five thousand hounds, having erected large kennels in Milan. As there was not room for all of them in this place many had to be boarded out in the neighbourhood. They were inspected once a fortnight by an officer called *Uffizio di cani*. If the dogs were too lean the keepers of them them were punished, if they were too fat they were punished also ; if one of them died, the keeper lost all his property. No one was allowed to keep dogs except Bernabò, and the game laws were enforced with the most terrible penalties. Bernabò gradually became more cruel as he grew older, but the administration of his kingdom shows great ability. We might, as a contrast to these horrors, give an account of the splendour of the feasts and banquets which we find side by side with these incredible horrors. No disgust at the inhumanity of the court and government of the Visconti seems to have prevented them from being accepted as welcome friends to sovereign princes. In 1365 Bernabò married his daughter Verde to Leopold, Duke of Austria. In 1368 Violante degli Visconti, daughter of Galeazzo, was married to Lionel, Duke of Clarence, son of Edward III. of England. She received the town of Alba for her dowry, and it was there that the Duke of Clarence died. In 1368, at the birth of Valentina, the daughter of Gian Galeazzo, who afterwards became Duchess of Orleans, festivities, which lasted for many days, were attended by Amadeo of Savoy, Niccolò of Este, and Malatesta of Rimini.

It may be asked how the Visconti managed to obtain such undisputed power in a city which preserved at least the tradition of popular government. It was much in the same way that the early emperors of Rome consolidated their authority, by grasping powers which were in their origin democratic, transforming them into a despotism, and throwing all other offices into the shade. The usual heads of the government in an Italian town were the *capitano del popolo* and the *podestà*—one invested with executive, the other with judicial, authority. The power of one of these magistrates varied inversely with that of the other. When party spirit ran high, and one party largely predominated, the *capitano*, as the head of the victorious party, would naturally be supreme, being only controlled by the principal members of the party which he led. The post of *capitano del popolo* might be taken by two other officers. Either the town, weary of the perpetual dissensions of party, might submit themselves to a *signore*, whose authority was defined by a *concordat* differing in different cases; or the emperor might call into being a claim long dormant, but never dead, and appoint an imperial vicar. When the citizens ceased to fight for themselves, and employed mercenaries, the hiring of these troops gave opportunity to the *signore* to amass a large fortune. A further step was taken when several towns chose the same *signore*. He was more independent of each of them. The property of traitors was confiscated for his private purse; his conquests were made as much for himself as the towns he ruled over. Some districts were made entirely subject to military rule. A *fiscus* or private purse of the princes grew up beside the *aerarium* or public treasury of the state. Thus the popular supremacy was changed into a military despotism. Still the republican forces did not cease altogether to exist, and they were always ready to start into life when the overmastering force, which kept them down, should be removed.

We have already related how, in 1367, Urban V. returned

for a short time to Rome, and met there the two Emperors of
the East and the West. He also formed a powerful league
which was at first directed against the bands of mercenary
soldiers, the *compagnie della ventura*, who were devastating
the land, but was afterwards used to crush the Visconti.
The Florentines and the della Scala refused to join this
confederacy.   The Visconti took care to ally themselves
with the house of Bavaria and the royal house of England, and this last alliance secured to them the assistance
of John Hawkwood. The war broke out in 1368, and
lasted only a few months. It was principally concentrated round Mantua, and was put an end to by the
weakness of the Emperor Charles. About this time the
union between the two brothers had become weakened.
Galeazzo went to live in Pavia, while Bernabò remained in
Milan. Another short war, in which the Florentines took
part with the league, broke out in 1369, but came to an
end in November 1370. The events which led to the restoration of the seat of the papacy to Italy wrought a change
in the position of the Visconti. Gregory XI. began by
excommunicating the tyrants of Milan, as his predecessor
had done, and found no difficulty in stirring up against
them the jealousy and vengeance of their neighbours and
rivals. But a great alteration took place when Florence,
as has been already related, put herself at the head of a
general rising against the papal power in Italy. She did
not hesitate to call Bernabò Visconti to her assistance.
Galeazzo had, in 1375, made over the greater part of his
dominions to his son Gian Galeazzo, the Conte di Virtù.
He himself took no part in the anti-papal league, but, on
the contrary, made peace with the pope, and sent him
money. Gregory, being anxious to settle in Italy, was

desirous for peace. He arranged a marriage between the Marquis of Montferrat and Violante, the widow of the Duke of Clarence. Therefore, when Galeazzo died in 1378, he was able to leave his son Gian Galeazzo at peace with all the world. We shall return again to the closing years of Bernabò, who died in 1385. Notwithstanding the inhuman and almost incredible cruelties of Galeazzo Visconti, he was a great patron of literature and the arts. He founded the University of Pavia in 1361, he summoned to his side the great teachers of Europe; and Petrarch the poet, the incarnation of the highest culture of his time, was admitted to an equal footing with the princes of the blood. The creation of the Certosa of Pavia, the most beautiful of all Carthusian monasteries, is a proof of his consummate taste, even if it should rather be regarded as a monument of his remorse.

We have seen in the last chapter that Gregory VI. returned to Rome in 1377. His first object was to make peace with the principal powers that were in rebellion against him. St Catherine of Siena laboured to effect a peace between the pope and the Florentines, but was unable to effect anything. The pope placed the city of Florence under an interdict, but the Signory ordered the churches to be reopened. The pope was more fortunate in making terms with Bologna and with Francesco, prefect of Vico, son of the famous Giovanni. At last Bernabò Visconti was chosen to mediate between Florence and the pope, and determined to get a share of the profits for himself. A congress was summoned to Sarzana at the beginning of 1378, in which the Florentines, the pope, and the king of France were represented. Bernabò, for his own interests, tried to impose harsh terms on the Florentines, but the business of the congress was interrupted by the sudden death of the pope on March 27, 1378. The congress was broken up, and a new era opened for the Church. The "Babylonian Captivity" had just come to an end, but the Church was disturbed for another fifty years by the "Great Schism," during which two rival popes stood opposed to each other, and divided the allegiance of the Christian world.

On the death of Gregory XI. the Church possessed twenty-three cardinals, of whom six were in Avignon, one was cardinal legate in Tuscany. Sixteen came together in conclave at Rome ; of these, eleven were French, four Italian, and one Spanish. The French cardinals were also divided into two parties—the Limousin cardinals, created by Popes Clement and Gregory, and the rest. The Limousin cardinals were in favour of electing a pope outside the sacred college, in the person of Bartolommeo Prignani, Archbishop of Bari. He was a Neapolitan by birth, was devoted to queen Johanna, had lived long in Avignon, and seemed to unite the conflicting claims of Italy and France. This view was generally supported by the other cardinals, notably by Pietro da Luna of Arragon, who afterwards became Benedict XIII. The cardinals went into conclave on the evening of April 7. As they entered, the people crowded round them with cries of "*Papa Romano volemo*" —"We wish for a Roman pope." The magistrates of the city made the same demand. That night there was a tumult in the city, which frightened the cardinals very much. The election took place the next evening. The Cardinal of Florence voted for the cardinal of San Pietro, all the rest gave their suffrage to the Archbishop of Bari. But they were afraid to publish what they had done. They first recited the "hours," and then they had dinner, while the crowd was bawling outside, " We want a pope, we want a Roman pope." After dinner they proceeded to a new election, when the Archbishop of Bari was unanimously chosen. Still they were afraid to make it known. The mob surged around the palaces, and the cardinals were afraid that they would be treated with personal violence. Cardinal Orsini now looked out of a window and cried, " Andate a San Pietro "—" Go to St Peter's." The mob, thinking that the cardinal of St Peter had been elected, according to ancient customs pillaged his house, and consumed all the provisions collected for the consumption of the conclave. The cardinals fled for safety in all directions. The newly-elected pope cowered in fear in the recesses of the Vatican. However, on the following day the election of the Bishop of Bari was formally declared, he was crowned in the church of St John Lateran, and the cardinals returned to Rome. There can be no doubt that he was legally and properly consecrated pope.

Urban VI. began his reign by making some necessary reforms, but in so hasty and impetuous a manner that he alienated all his friends. He limited the cardinals to one dish at dinner, he excommunicated those guilty of simony, he declared that he would not leave Rome, and that he would fill the sacred college with Italian and Roman cardinals. He was also regarded as a terrible man, capable of anything. The Italian cardinals were with the pope at Tivoli, the French cardinals were at Anagni, and they refused to attend a consistory at Tivoli to consider the legitimacy of the pope's title. At last the French cardinals were brought to regret that they had consented to the election of an Italian pope. They removed from Anagni to Fondi, and on August 9

declared that Urban VI. had been improperly elected
under the constraint of popular tumult. On December 20,
1378, they elected as pope Robert, son of Amadeo III.,
bishop of Cambray, who took the name of Clement VII.
In the meantime Urban had appointed twenty-nine new
Italian cardinals. The catholic world was divided between
the two pontiffs. France, Spain, and Naples recognised
Clement VII. ; the rest of Italy, Germany, Scandinavia,
England, Hungary, Poland, and Portugal gave their allegiance to Urban VI.

In one of the consistories held at Tivoli Pope Urban
VI. had made peace with Florence in terms more advantageous than those which had been proposed at Sarzana.
But the same year witnessed the outbreak of a revolution at Florence more violent than any which has been
already mentioned. In order to make it intelligible it
will be necessary to go back to the period of the peace
between Florence and Pisa in 1364. The power of
the *ammonire*, by which any citizens who were dis-
pleasing to the ruling faction could be excluded from
power, established in 1351, had been used in a most
unsparing manner by the rich commercial nobles, at the
head of whom stood the family of the Albizzi. They
were opposed, as has been stated above, by the family
of the Ricci, who, of lower rank themselves, now joined
by some of the *grandi*, and by the *popolo minuto*, and
especially by the *ciompi*, the lower artisans who were
not organised in guilds. The strife between the Albizzi
and the Ricci had been so violent, that in 1372
measures were taken for excluding the heads of both
parties from power for five years. The *Otto di guerra*,
established in 1376, united themselves with the Ricci party,

and being at war with the pope, and in alliance with the Visconti, may be regarded as to some extent penetrated with Ghibelline sympathies. They stood, therefore, in sharp opposition to the *Capitani di parte Guelfa*, and the family of the Albizzi, and these were supported by the *popolo minuto*. In 1378 the bags containing the names of candidates for office were nearly empty, the few names that remained in them belonged to the Ricci party. The Albizzi knew that in the next *balià* which was held to fill them, their adversaries would probably have the upper hand, and that they would be excluded from office for a number of years, just as they in their turn had excluded their enemies. They were particularly afraid lest Salvestro de' Medici should become *gonfaloniere* of justice. The lot, however, fell in his favour, and he became *gonfaloniere* for the months of May and June.

In the Florentine constitution, the rule about the initiation of new measures was peculiar. The *gonfaloniere*, and each of the eight *priors*, held in turn the office of *proposto*, and this officer alone had the power of submitting any measure to the vote, whoever might have suggested the measure in the first instance. On June 18, Salvestro de' Medici, being *proposto*, proposed to the *collegio*, that is, to the *priori*, the sixteen *gonfalonieri di compagnia*, and the twelve *buoni uomini*, that the ordinances of justice should be enforced strictly against the *grandi*, that the powers of the *capitani di parte Guelfa* should be cut down, and that certain *ammoniti* should again be admitted to office. When the *collegio* hesitated to pass these propositions, Salvestro broke into the *consiglio del popolo*, who were sitting in the lower floor, and complained that what he suggested was for the advantage of the State, and that he had not been allowed to carry his measures. There was a general uproar, the square below was full of soldiers, who owed allegiance to the *otto di guerra;* the *collegio* being intimidated, gave way, and the ordinances of justice were re-established for one year. There was a second disturbance on June 22, in consequence of which a *balía*, or committee of eighty persons, including the *collegio* and the *otto di guerra*, was appointed to reform the constitution. Many attempts were made to effect this, but they were all inadequate. Salvestro de' Medici saw that stronger measures were necessary. He united himself with the *ciompi*, who determined to gain by violence what they could not get by milder means. Their plans were hastened by fear of discovery.

On July 20, at daybreak, the whole city was in arms. The insurgents burnt the house of Luigi Guicciardini, who had succeeded Salvestro de' Medici as *gonfaloniere ;* they seized the sacred banner itself, and carried it through the streets, destroying and pillaging as they went. The *ciompi* presented a petition, demanding to be included in the government. This was approved of by the *collegio*, but had not yet been submitted to the council of the people. The mob now attacked the palace of justice, crying out, "Come down all of you, and be off with you, we will not have any more *signori*." The priors and the rest of the government yielded to the cry, and the palace was in the possession of the people. It happened that the *gonfalone* of justice was carried up the great staircase by a poor wool-carder, with ragged clothes and bare feet, called Michele Lando. By a spontaneous impulse he was summoned to the post of *gonfaloniere*. He might have used his power to increase the anarchy for his private ends, but he really employed it to give tranquillity to the city. He deposed all the existing magistrates, burned the bags which contained the names of future officers, and formed a *signoria* from the *arti maggiori*, the *arti minori*, and the *popolo minuto*. He made the people lay down their arms, attacked the *ciompi*, and put them to flight. On August 31 he laid down his office, having restored peace and quiet to the city. The *ciompi* gained nothing by this outbreak. The people, when they had recovered from their excitement, refused to admit the *popolo minuto* to power. The *signoria* was to be drawn in future from the seven greater *arti* and the sixteen lesser in the proportion of four to five. The result of this revolution was to place the power in the hands of Salvestro de' Medici and his friends. The heads of the old Guelph party were exiled, and the leaders of the *ciompi* as well, with the exception of Lando, who was treated as a hero. Florence remained quiet for some years without further disturbance.

CHAPTER XIV.

QUEEN JOHANNA OF NAPLES—THE WAR OF CHIOGGIA—
THE PEACE OF TURIN.

THIS chapter will be occupied by two subjects which are
connected with each other in point of time, although they
have reference to the fortunes of different portions of the
Peninsula—the closing years of Johanna, queen of Naples,
and the war between Venice and Genoa, generally called
the war of Chioggia. Queen Johanna married four husbands
in succession. The first was Andrew of Hungary whose
tragical end was the cause of all her troubles. He was
murdered on September 20, 1345, after less than two years'
marriage. Just a year after his death she married Lewis of
Tarentum, her cousin, who died on May 25, 1362. On
January 12, 1363, she married James III. of the house of
Arragon, king of the island of Majorca. After his death
she again remained a widow for a year, when she married
Otto, Duke of Brunswick, who was guardian to the sons
of the Marquis of Montferrat. She had a child by her first
husband who was taken to Hungary and died there shortly
afterwards. She was now old and childless, and her heir
was a distant cousin. His genealogy cannot be made intelligible without some attention. Charles of Anjou, the
conqueror of Naples, had four sons—Charles Martel,
Robert, Lewis, and John—founders, respectively, of the

houses of Hungary, Naples, Tarentum and Durazzo. The house of Durazzo split up into two parts, the younger of which was called the house of Gravina, and the representative of this house, and heir to the crown of Naples, was Charles of Gravina, great-grandson of Charles of Anjou, second cousin of Johanna. He was married to the only other claimant to the Neapolitan throne, his cousin Margaret, daughter of Charles, Duke of Durazzo. Charles of Gravina was educated at the Hungarian court, and served in the Hungarian army.

Johanna had incurred the hatred and vengeance of Pope Urban VI. by the support which she had given to his rival Clement VII. He therefore declared her incapable of reigning, and offered the crown of Naples to Charles of Gravina. Charles was at this time engaged as the general of the king of Hungary in the war of Chioggia against the Venetians of which we shall presently give an account. Johanna looked around for some assistance in her difficulties, and naturally turned her eyes to that same house of France from which she was herself sprung, and which we find throughout the course of our history constantly interfering with Italian affairs. She chose as her heir Lewis of Anjou —who was connected with the royal family of France in the following manner. Lewis VIII. of France, who died in 1226, had three sons, Lewis IX., commonly called St Lewis, Robert of Artois, and Charles of Anjou. Charles was the founder of the first house of Anjou, which we have seen seated on the throne of Naples. St Lewis, his elder brother, had four sons—Philippe le Hardi, Robert of Bourbon, John of Valois, and Peter of Alençon. The crown passed to Charles of Valois, son of Philippe le Hardi, and brother of Philippe le Bel. He married as his first wife, Margaret,

Princess of Naples in Anjou, and took the title of Count of Anjou. His two successors, Philip VI. and John II., were both Counts of Anjou. After the death of John, the county of Anjou became again separated from the crown, and passed to his son Lewis, who was the founder of the second house of Anjou. The other sons of John were Charles V., who became king, John of Berri, and Philip the Bold, founder of the second and greater house of Burgundy, who married Margaret, Countess of Flanders, Duchess of Brabant, and thus obtained the Low Countries for the house of Austria. Johanna, in her extremity, determined to make this Lewis of Anjou her heir.

Charles of Durazzo marched southward from the Venetian territory to claim his dominions. He received little encouragement from the Florentines, who had always been well disposed to Johanna, as the daughter of their former Lord, King Robert of Naples ; and they were afraid of the consequence of uniting the crowns of Naples and Hungary on the same head. In Rome, Charles received the crown of Naples from the pope on conditions similar to those on which it had been given to his ancestor, Charles of Anjou. It was provided that the pope's nephew should receive fiefs in the Neapolitan territory. Charles entered his kingdom in the spring of 1381. Otto of Brunswick prepared to oppose him, but was forced to retire, and Charles occupied the capital without opposition. Queen Johanna was shut up in the Castello Nuovo. She had not enough provisions for herself and her suite, and her husband was unable to succour her. In an attempt to relieve the castle, he was taken prisoner, and his ward, the young Duke of Montferrat, was killed. Johanna was forced to surrender herself, and on May 22, 1382, she was murdered—smothered, it is said, under a feather bed.

Lewis of Hungary was still alive to enjoy the tardy punishment of the murderer of his brother. Lewis of Anjou hastened to avenge the death of his benefactress. After the death of his brother Charles V. he had become guardian of the infant King Charles VI., and Regent of France. Accompanied by the Counts of Savoy and Geneva, and by a number of French nobles, he entered the Abruzzi in July 1382. The Neapolitan barons who had remained faithful to the party of Johanna, joined his standard. From this time forth, we find in Naples a civil strife between the factions of Anjou and Hungary, which reduced the kingdom of Naples to a worse condition of misery than before. It is scarcely worth while to recount the events of the war in detail. The Count of Anjou died of fever at Biseglia on October 10, 1384, and his army was dispersed. His death did not give peace to the kingdom, for the barons of the Anjou party continued the struggle, and, strange to say, they were joined by the pope, who had invited Charles of Durazzo into Italy. Charles could not put up with the fiery and arrogant temper of Urban VI. He went so far as to besiege him in the castle of Nocera, and the Pope was forced to take refuge in Genoa. In the meantime, King Lewis of Hungary had died in 1382, after a reign of forty years. His daughter Maria was married to Sigismund, Margrave of Brandenburg, second son of Charles VI., and afterwards emperor. Maria laid claim to the throne of Hungary, but a large party were in favour of Charles of Durazzo, and he was recalled from Italy in September 1396. On his arrival he was recognised as king, and placed on the throne, but was shortly afterwards treacherously murdered by the queen in February 1296. Thus the kingdom of Hungary, like that of Naples, became the scene of hopeless anarchy. Margaret, the widow of Charles of Durazzo, reigned in Naples as guardian of her young son Ladislaus. Mary of Blois, the widow of Lewis of Anjou, retired with her young son Lewis II. into Provence, to wait for a season of revenge. At a later period these elements of discord broke out again into open war.

The war of Chioggia, as it is called, between Venice and Genoa, is the fourth war which took place between these two rival maritime powers. The Greek Empire was at this time tottering under the assaults of the Turks, but the sceptre of Constantinople was still feebly held by John Palæologus. Sunk in apathy and debauch, he had imprisoned and attempted to blind his son and grandson, Andronicus and John. They were released by the Genoese, and their eyesight was in some measure recovered. The Genoese now attempted to place Andronicus on the throne, while the Venetians took the side of his father John. The island of Tenedos, which had been ceded by Andronicus to his friends, became the bone of contention, being attacked by the Genoese and defended by the Venetians. The island of Cyprus belonged at this time to the family of Lusignan. In 1372 a new king was to be crowned in the Cathedral of Nicosia. The Venetians and Genoese strove for precedence at the ceremony, and it was given to the Venetians. The Genoese attempted force; a rising took place, and all the Genoese in the island were massacred. This naturally formed a second cause of quarrel. Each side had powerful allies. Genoa was joined by the king of Hungary, the Patriarch of Aquileia, and Francesco Carrara, lord of Padua; the king of Cyprus and Bernabò Visconti took the side of Venice. Space does not permit us to give a full account of the events of the war. It raged most furiously around the island of Chioggia in the autumn of 1378 and the spring of 1380.

Venice is built on a number of islands lying amongst shallow lagoons, and defended from the open sea by a natural belt of sand, called the Lido, and a strong sea-wall. At one of the entrances of this defence lies the town of Chioggia, which still possesses for the eye of the traveller some of the characteristics of Venice in the middle ages. Pietro Doria assisted by Francesco of Carrara, attacked this town and took it, and the Venetians heard with alarm that their enemies were established at twenty-five miles' distance from themselves. This was the greatest danger which had befallen the republic since its foundation. The inhabitants crowded round the Doge Andreo Contarini and compelled him to sue for peace. A piece of white paper was offered to Francis of Carrara on which he might write his own terms, but Doria haughtily answered that he would grant no peace until with his own hands he had bridled the bronze horses, which from the porch of the cathedral dominate the Square of St Mark. This answer roused the people to new exertions. At the news of the capture of Chioggia an Hungarian army invaded the territory of Treviso, while the Paduans made several conquests on the Venetian *terra firma*. Lewis of Hungary refused to trust his allies unless he was allowed to fly his own banner at the side of the winged lion of St Mark, and unless the Venetians agreed to pay him tribute, and to accept his consent as necessary for the confirmation of a Doge.

The Genoese fleet now advanced still nearer; it came as far as San Niccolò del Lido, and even threatened to attack Venice itself. The people turned in their distress to the

only man who could save them. Vettor Pisani, who had
been imprisoned after his defeat at Polà, was now set at
liberty and placed in command. He fortified all the canals
and passages from the open sea. The richest families of
Venice contributed their wealth and their children to the
defence of their country. It was made known that thirty
of the *popolani* who had shown themselves most deserving
should be enrolled in the Great Council at the close of the
war. In the meantime, Carlo Zeno, a Venetian admiral,
who had run the blockade of the Genoese fleet, had attacked
the sea-board of Genoa, burnt Porto Venere, and picking up
some reinforcements on his way, had sailed to Constantinople
and restored John Palæologus to the throne. He was
in the waters of Cyprus when he heard of the loss of
Chioggia, and of his recall. Vettor Pisani, having carefully
trained his fleet, now thought that Zeno could not be far
off, and that the moment for the attack had come. On the
evening of December 23, 1379, he set sail with more than
thirty galleys. The aged Doge Andrea Contarini, now
more than seventy years old, and weak in health, went in
person on board the galleys, having taken an oath that he
would not return unless he were victorious. With great
difficulty the Venetians succeeded in closing the channels
on either side of the island of Chioggia. But their situation
was most precarious. Provisions were beginning to fail, and
their galleys were fully exposed to the Genoese fire. The
Doge was obliged to say that unless Zeno made his appearance before the first of January 1380 he would be
obliged to raise the siege. In that case it had been determined that Venice should be deserted and that the seat
of Government should be transferred to Candia. On the very
day fixed as the term of their exertions the expected help

arrived. On the morning of January 1, Carlo Zeno appeared with munitions and supplies. The Venetians were now able to attack Chioggia by land. Pietro Doria, the Genoese admiral, was killed at Brondolo on February 3, and his place was occupied by Gaspare Spinola. The Genoese were driven within the walls of Chioggia, and anxiously expected assistance. Vettor Pisani contrived to prevent any aid from approaching, and in the middle of June the Genoese sued for peace. Five thousand prisoners and thirty-two galleys fell into the hands of the conquerors.

But although Chioggia was recovered, the war was not at an end. The treasury of St Mark was exhausted, and the Venetians had to contend on all sides with their enemies. Vettor Pisani, the idol of the sailors, died at Manfredonia, and Carlo Zeno was appointed to succeed him. Treviso had to be surrendered, the last important possession of Venice on the *terra firma*. Trieste had already rebelled and placed itself under the protection of the patriarch of Aquileia. At last, by the intervention of Amadeus VI. of Savoy, the peace of Turin was concluded on August 6, 1381. It consisted of four separate treaties. By the treaty between Venice and Hungary it was agreed that the Venetians should pay to the crown of Hungary seven thousand ducats every year; that the Hungarians on their side should not sail on any river which disembogued into the Adriatic between Cape Palmentaria and Rimini, also that Dalmatian merchants should not buy goods in Venice to a greater value than 35,000 ducats. It was arranged between Venice and Genoa that the island of Tenedos was to be delivered to the Count of Savoy, and made uninhabitable, all buildings being razed to the ground. The Venetians on their side, promised not to support the king of Cyprus. There remained Padua and Trieste. With the first, however, it was agreed that conquests should be surrendered on both sides, and with the second, that Trieste should be free, paying a yearly tribute to the Doge. The general results of the war had been to deprive the Venetians of their possessions on the mainland and to destroy the fleet and the resources of Genoa. The promise was kept of admitting thirty families into the Great Council as a reward for their patriotism.

CHAPTER XV.

GÏAN GALEAZZO VISCONTI—LADISLAUS—THE COUNCIL OF PISA.

THE history of Venice in the decade which followed the peace of Turin, is closely united with the future of the great cities of the Lombard plain—Padua, Verona, and Milan. Padua was governed from 1355 to 1382 by Francesco of Carrara, the seventh of his family who had been lords of that city. We have already heard of him as a bitter and successful enemy of Venice. He had already attained possession of Treviso, and was anxious to extend his dominions westward towards the frontiers of Verona. This town was ruled by Antonio della Scala, an illegitimate scion of that famous house. His descent from the line of Scaligers was as follows: Mastino II., who had been lord of Verona from 1329 to 1357, left three sons, Cangrande, Alboin, and Cansignorio. The eldest was murdered by his brother after a reign of seven years, and Alboin and Cansignorio reigned together. In 1365 Alboin was detected in a conspiracy, and was put to death by his brother Cansignorio, who reigned alone. Dying in 1375, he left his dominions to his two illegitimate sons, Bartolommeo and Antonio, who divided his dominions between them. But this arrangement only led to another fractricide, and from 1381 to 1387 Antonio reigned alone. He had been alarmed at the

progress of Francesco da Carrara, and had joined the
Venetians in making war against him. His generals were
defeated, and his rival was quite willing to offer him terms
of peace which he rejected. He had now to make head
against a new enemy in the person of Gian Galeazzo
Visconti, to a description of whose career this chapter will
be devoted.

We have already heard how the territory of Milan came
to be divided between Galeazzo and Bernabò Visconti.
Galeazzo died in 1378, and was succeeded by his son
Gian Galeazzo, Count of Vertus, husband of Isabelle of
France. Bernabò, in his old age, divided his territory
amongst his five sons, retaining the general superintendence
of it for himself. This naturally aroused the jealousy of
Gian Galeazzo, who, on the other hand, excited that of his
uncle by being appointed Imperial Vicar by the Emperor
Wenceslaus, son of Charles IV. Gian Galeazzo adopted an
ingenious and characteristic way of disarming his uncle's
suspicion. As his wife had died leaving no children, he
married Catherine, daughter of Bernabò, and gave his sister
Violante in marriage to Bernabò's son. He took care that
his government should be a striking contrast to that of his
uncle; he reformed the criminal justice, lightened taxa-
tion, paid honour to the clergy, and deserted the traditional
methods of severity and harshness on which the power of
an Italian tyrant was supposed to rest. Bernabò, on the
other hand, became more savage in his old age, and more
enslaved by disgraceful vices. He thought his nephew no
better than a coward and a fool, and may possibly have
conceived the design of removing him and succeeding to
his inheritance. If this was the case Gian Galeazzo
contrived to be beforehand with him. He put on

more and more the air of harmless simplicity. He
lived at Pavia, and devoted himself to science and to
the company of learned men; he spent incredible
sums in almsgiving, sang hymns with the monks, and
remained for hours in prayer, until Bernabò thought him
positively mad. At last in 1385 he wrote to his uncle
that he wished to make a pilgrimage to our Lady of the
Mountain at Varese, that he should pass by Milan, but
was afraid to enter the town; would his uncle meet him and
allow him to embrace him? He set out with a guard of 500
lances. Bernabò had been warned against him, but would
believe nothing. On the road to Milan he met two of his
uncle's sons, whom he made prisoners. At a little distance
from the city he was met by Bernabò himself. Gian Galeazzo
gave an order to his attendants in German. Jacobo del
Verme the famous *condottiere*, who accompanied Gian
Galeazzo said to Bernabò, "You are a prisoner," and the
nephew made his entry into Milan amidst the acclamations
and applause of the people. In three weeks he became
undisputed master of all Bernabò's possessions. Bernabò
was imprisoned in the magnificent castle of Trezzo, which
he had built, circled by the folds of the green and rushing
Adda, and was poisoned on December 19. He died
repeating the words—"A humble and a contrite heart,
O God, thou wilt not despise." He was sixty-six years old.

The first act of Gian Galeazzo's rule was to form a league
with the Este, Cararra, and Gonzaghi, for the extermination of
the mercenaries who were devastating Italy. The banner of
the Confederation was a blue ensign with the inscription
"Pax." This dream lasted but a short time, for personal
selfishness and ambition soon scattered it to the winds.
Gian Galeazzo could not resist the bait of Verona which

M

was offered him, and he accepted the offer of Francesco de Carrara to join with him against Antonio della Scala. It was agreed that in case of success he should receive the town of Verona ; Carrara was to have Vicenza. Antonio was entirely defeated, and Visconti, with characteristic cunning, managed to get possession of both towns. This was the end of the house of La Scala, which had been lords of Verona for a hundred and twenty-eight years. Gian Galeazzo having mortally offended Carrara by taking possession of Vicenza, had now the incredible baseness to join Venice in a league against him. He had previously strengthened his position by marrying his only daughter Valentina to Lewis, Duke of Orleans, the brother of Charles VI. of France, giving her as a dowry Asti and the other possessions of the Visconti in Piedmont. From this marriage was descended Lewis XII., King of France, who claimed the duchy of Milan in the beginning of the sixteenth century. A treaty was signed between Gian Galeazzo and Venice in February 1388. It provided that Padua should belong to the Visconti, but that the fortifications should be razed ; he was also to conquer Treviso and hand it over to the Republic : further, he was to pay a large sum for the support of the war. Carrara, believing that the Venetians were chiefly actuated by personal hatred against himself, abdicated his sovereignty and retired to Treviso. He was succeeded by his son Francesco Novello. But father and son were forced to submit. They surrendered themselves under a safe conduct which was treacherously broken, and the dragon of the Visconti floated over the walls of Padua and Treviso within sight of the canals of Venice. Visconti had, as we have seen, already reduced to vassalage the Marquis of Montferrat, the Gonzaghi of Mantua, and the Este of Ferrara.

In Tuscany alone could be found a counterpoise to this overgrown and monstrous power founded on fraud and violence. Francesco Novello had been sent by Gian Galeazzo to a castle in the territory of Asti, with the intention of putting him to death. He contrived to escape, and passing with his wife and child through incredible dangers and difficulties, he scoured Europe to reek revenge against the enemy of his race. Repulsed and threatened everywhere, he was well received at Florence, and was charged to collect an army in Germany. He was welcomed by the Duke of Bavaria, and then passed into Croatia and Bosnia, where he received the promise of powerful assistance. It is possible that the Florentines might after all have hesitated before attacking so powerful a foe as the lord of Milan, but Gian Galeazzo removed all possibility of this by being himself the first to attack. In the spring of 1390 he declared war against Bologna and Florence. The Republic took John Hawkwood into their pay, but unfortunately they were not seconded by their old allies of the Guelphic quadrilateral. Siena and Perugia were on the side of Visconti, as also were the lords of Urbino, Faenza, Rimini, Forlì, and Tivoli. The Milanese army was too much scattered to be of any use. Francesco of Carrara, advancing from the north, entered his native city of Padua by the dry bed of the Brenta, as Cyrus, in past times, had entered Babylon. Here he received the reinforcements of the Duke of Bavaria. The Florentines found a powerful auxiliary in John, Count of Armagnac, whose sister had married an uncle of Bernabò Visconti. Whilst he attacked on the side of Piedmont, John Hawkwood had crossed the Mincio and the Oglio, and was encamped on the banks of the Adda. The Count of Armagnac, a young man of eight and twenty, was defeated by Jacopo del Verme, Visconti's general at Alessandria, and Hawkwood was exposed to the full fury of the victor's attack. There was nothing left for him but to retreat. He was reduced to terrible straits, at one time he was surrounded by a waste of floods, which del Verme had caused by cutting the dykes of the Po. He escaped by marching a day and part of the night with the floods up to the horses' bellies. At last, when both parties were tired of war, the peace of Genoa was concluded on January 20, 1392. Padua was restored to the house of Carrara, but Novello was compelled to pay a tribute of ten thousand florins to Milan; the Florentines were to abstain from interference in Lombardy, and Gian Galeazzo equally from interference in Tuscany.

With so restless a spirit as Gian Galeazzo, peace could not last long. In 1393 he conceived the idea of ruining Mantua by turning the course of the Mincio, and draining the lakes which are the principal defence of that city. Gonzaga applied to Florence and Bologna for assistance. The possession of Ferrara supplied a cause of further quarrel. At this juncture the Emperor Wenceslaus entered upon the scene. His chief object was to obtain money, and he thought that he might gain what he wished by heading a league against Gian Galeazzo. Finding this to be impracticable, he sold to the lord of Milan the title of duke. On May 1, 1395, by a decree signed at Prague, he erected the town and diocese of Milan into an imperial fief or duchy. The investiture was celebrated with great pomp and splendour. The new duchy included Brescia, Bergamo, Vercelli, Como, Novara, Alessandria, Tortona, Bobbio, Piacenza, Reggio, Parma, Cremona, Lodi, Crema, Soncino, Bormio, Borgo San Donnino, Pontremoli, Verona, Vicenza,

Feltre, Belluno, Bassano, and Sarzana. Pavia was formed into a separate county. This diploma, which cost Gian Galeazzo a hundred thousand florins, gave an entirely new position to the Visconti. They were no longer tyrants of a city, but the hereditary sovereigns of a considerable territory.

The first use which Gian Galeazzo made of the new power which he had acquired, was to attach himself to the league which had been made for the purpose of his overthrow. In May 1396 a congress of the league was held in Florence. Not only were the members willing to receive the duke as an ally, but the people of Siena, of Lucca, and of Rimini joined the new confederation, which thus entirely lost the original character which it had received from Francesco da Gonzaga. This unnatural state of things could not last long. Jealousy of the duke's power was too deep-seated and too well-founded that his enemies should not combine to crush it. The Visconti had in former days held the signory of Genoa, and Gian Galeazzo saw in the distractions of that city an opportunity of gaining the authority which they had once possessed. But Charles VI., king of France, who was as yet untouched by the malady which at a later period destroyed his intellect, had his eyes fixed on the same prize. Adorno, Doge of Genoa, preferred the alliance of France to that of Milan, and Charles, finding that his interests clashed with those of the Visconti, stirred up a conspiracy against him. In September 1396 a league was concluded at Paris, by which Florence, Bologna, Ferrara, Mantua, and Padua were to devote themselves to the destruction of their common foe. Gian Galeazzo was not slow to meet the danger. He despatched the famous *condottiere*, Alberico da Barbiano, to attack the town of San Miniato, even before the Florentines had formally declared war. But the duke recognised that his most formidable and determined enemy was Francesco of Gonzaga, and against him he sent two armies. As he was defended by no one except the Marquis of Este, his destruction appeared certain. But his very weakness proved his strength. Venice and the League could not notice the unbounded development of the power of Milan with indifference. They took the part of Mantua, and Visconti was defeated at the battle of Governolo. This at first only increased the obstinacy of the duke, and aroused him to new efforts. He wrenched still larger taxes from his oppressed people, and took new *condottieri* into his pay. But the power of the Venetians was too great for him. By their influence a peace for ten years was concluded in May 1398.

Gian Galeazzo had now leisure to turn his attention to Tuscany. Pisa was in the hands of Jacopo Appiano, an old man of seventy-five. The duke thought that he would be able to cajole him into surrendering the city into his hands, but the spirit of resistance was too strong, and his envoys were repulsed. Appiano unfortunately died on September 5, and his successor was of a different stamp. The Florentines refused to assist him in the tyranny which he contemplated to establish, and he therefore sold the town of Pisa to Gian Galeazzo for two hundred thousand florins, the Pisans in vain protesting against being sold like a flock of sheep. The duke took possession of the city, and the house of Appiano had to content itself with Piombino and Elba, where it long continued to reign. Gian Galeazzo only considered these possessions as the point of departure for new conquests. The lords of the castle of Poppi, and the whole of the Casentino declared in his favour, so that the sources of the Arno, as well as its mouth, were hostile to the city which claimed the title of its queen. Hatred against the Florentines drove the people of Siena to commit their signory to the duke. Perugia felt herself hard pressed by the pope, and expected to find a milder ruler in Gian Galeazzo. Assissi followed the fate of Perugia. The power of the Duke of Milan extended itself over Spoleto and Nocera, and he had also obtained the dominions of the Malespina in the territory of the Lunigiana. He might well aspire to be king of Italy. At the close of the fourteenth century the outlook of freedom in Italy was indeed gloomy enough. Genoa, Perugia, and Siena had given themselves masters, Pisa had been sold, Lucca and Bologna, with the appearance of freedom, were distracted by party quarrels which were the fore-runners of servitude. Venice, defended by her lagoons, seemed willing to abandon Italy to her fate; Rome languished in slavery; Naples and Lombardy had forgotten the name of liberty. A cowardly and faithless tyrant had risen to the height of power by trading on the vice and weakness of his enemies. Florence alone upheld the standard of the good cause, and her eventual success is an encouragement to all true-hearted lovers of liberty not to despair even in the deepest abandonment and desolation.

In the season of her lowest abasement Florence had again reason to hope for the advent of a deliverer from beyond the Alps. The Emperor Wenzel, or Wenceslaus, was the son of the Emperor Charles IV. He had been nominated king of Bohemia at the age of two, and when he was crowned king of Germany at Aix-la-Chapelle in 1376 he was only fifteen years of age, and already married. In character he was nothing better than a drunken sot, a sad falling off from the chivalrous virtues of his grandfather John, and his great-grandfather Henry. He was sunk in idleness

and debauchery, and was quite unfit to attend to the most
necessary business. The princes of Germany had long been
discontented; one of their most serious grievances was
the creation of an independent duchy of Milan, and
the apparent surrender of one of the brightest jewels of
the imperial crown. They resolved to depose the unworthy emperor, but the princes of the Rhine first
summoned Wenceslaus to appear at the Castle of Ober-
lahnsbein on August 11, 1400. As might have been anticipated, he did not obey the summons; he was therefore
formally deposed nine days later at the solemn place of
election, Rense. The reasons assigned were, that he had
not appeased the schism in the churches as he ought to
have done, that he had dismembered the empire by erecting
Milan and Pavia into independent fiefs; that he failed to
secure the peace of his dominions; that he took no pains to
secure justice; and that he allowed prelates and priests to
be tortured and killed. On the following day Rupert III.,
the Palsgrave, or Count Palatine, was raised to the vacant
throne. He had already promised to put an end to the
papal schism, and to recover the territory of Milan for the
empire.

Rupert was poor and weak, and his authority was disputed;
he was therefore all the more anxious to begin his expedition
to Italy as soon as possible, in order that the pope might
crown him at Rome, and thus give his power a stability
which it did not now possess. Rupert sent envoys to the
Florentines, describing himself as the deadly enemy of Gian
Galeazzo, who had surpassed the enormity of his other crimes
by bribing Rupert's physician to poison him at Vienna.
The imperial army mustered at Augsburg in September
1401. The Florentines promised a sum of two hundred

thousand florins, on the condition that the independence of their town should be respected. From Innsbruck, on September 25, 1401, the emperor sent an order to Gian Galeazzo that he should surrender the imperial prisoners. At Trent, on October 14, Francesco of Carrara joined the advancing host with a reinforcement of two thousand cavalry. The whole number of German and Italian troops amounted to thirty-two thousand foot and horse. But these half disciplined German levies were ill suited to contend against the scientifically trained armies which fought under the banner of the Visconti, led by veteran *condottieri*. The decisive battle was fought at Brescia on October 24, and resulted in the complete defeat of the emperor. The day was won by the excellence of the Italian cavalry, an arm in which Rupert was deficient, as he had been obliged to send away five thousand cavalry from Innsbruck because he had not enough money to pay them. One onslaught was sufficient. Leopold of Austria was taken prisoner; the horse of Carrara alone held their ground, but Francesco their commander was so disgusted at the emperor's cowardice that he left him. Rupert returned disheartened and discredited to Trent.

Rupert did not dare to go to Germany with the disgrace of this failure upon him; he made his way through difficult mountain passes to Padua, where he was received by his old ally Francesco da Carrara. But the winter was at hand, and Carrara was soon tired of so troublesome and expensive a guest. The Florentines were unwilling to incur further risks, the Visconti were openly contemptuous, the pope made it a condition of the coronation that the emperor should not interfere with the matter of the schism. Supplies of money from Italy were failing; the debts contracted in Germany could not be paid. Rupert, pressed on all sides, was at last forced to retire to Germany. He returned there in April 1402, without an army, without money, and without honour. Gian Galeazzo took advantage of the retreat of the emperor to attack Bologna, which he regarded as a stepping-stone to the possession of Florence. He sent an army against the Bolognese, supported by the taxes which he had wrung out of the oppression of his subjects, under the command of Alberico da Barbiano. Giovanni de' Bentivogli, the lord of Bologna, allied himself with the houses of Padua and Florence, who knew that their own independence would be lost if Bologna should be enslaved. The two armies met at Casalvecchio on the Reno, a torrent which flows northward from the Appenines, to the Po, on St John's day, June 24, 1402. The Bolognese were entirely defeated, the city opened its gates to Alberico, the people received the representative of the Visconti with cries of *Viva il Duca, Morte al Bentivoglio*, and thus on July 10, 1402, Gian Galeazzo became lord of Bologna. He proceeded immediately to lay siege to Florence; he offered the towns of Feltre and Cividale to Venice as the price of his recognition as king of Italy, he went so far as to prepare his crown and royal robes, and settled the details of his triumphant entry into Florence, where he was to be crowned. But just as the prize was in his grasp it was dashed away by a more powerful hand. He fled from Pavia to avoid the plague, which was then raging in Italy, and took refuge at Melegnano, but the scourge seized him in the midst of his strongholds, and he died at the age of fifty-five on September 3, 1402. The death of the duke, the "great viper," as he was called from the cognisance on his coat of arms, gave joy to nearly the whole of Italy.

Gian Galeazzo left four sons, two legitimate—Giovanni

Maria, and Filippo Maria, and two illegitimate—Gabriele
Maria, and Giacomo. To the first he left, with the title of
Duke of Milan, Como, Bergamo, Brescia, Lodi, Cremona,
Piacenza, Parma, Reggio, Bologna, Siena, Perugia, Assisi;
to Filippa Maria, with the title of the Count of Pavia, and
the possession of that city, Tortona, Alessandria, Navara,
Vercelli, Casale, Valenza, Verona, Piacenza, Feltre, Cividale, and Belluno, Bassano and the Riviere di Trento; to
Gabrielle Maria, Pisa, Crema, and perhaps the Lunigiana.
As these children were all under age a Council of Regency
was appointed, of which the Duchess Caterina was the head,
and the members of which were the principal commanders
of the duke's army, Alberico, Jacopo del Verme, and others.
To these were added Pietro da Candia, the learned archbishop of Milan, who in 1409 was recognised as pope by
the name of Alexander V., and Francesco Barbarossa, the
duke's chamberlain and confidant. The duke had not considered what discontent and trouble would be caused by
associating a domestic servant in this intimate connection
with counsellors of higher rank. The death of the duke was
the signal for his enemies to attack. Pope Boniface IX.,
the Florentines, and the Marquis of Este formed a league
against the Visconti, and succeeded in attaching Alberico
to their side. The elevation of Barbarossa estranged
the friends of the Visconti, and alienated the people.
Ugo Cavalcabò became master of Cremona; Benzone of
Crema; Rusca of Como; Soardi of Bergamo; Vignoli of
Lodi. Brescia, Piacenza, and Bobbio were distracted with
civil war. Peace with the pope was bought by the sacrifice
of Bologna, Perugia, and Assisi. In the midst of their
distress the duchess determined upon a *coup d' état*. In
January 1404 she enticed the officers of the regency into

the castle in which she lived, threw them into prison, and
beheaded some of them ; she then recalled Barbarossa, who
had been driven from power in the previous June.   This
government did not last long ; before the end of the year
the duchess and her favourite were compelled to fly, and
she died of hunger on October 14, 1404.

In the general break-up of the Visconti's dominions, the
lords of the Lombard plain did not neglect their opportunity.   Francesco da Carrara, with whom the duchess had
at first intended to make peace, being irritated on account
of a breach of faith, laid siege to Verona.   Guglielmo
della Scala offered to give Vicenza to Carrara if he would
assist him in recovering the city of his ancestors.   Verona
was captured, and Guglielmo was restored, but he died
on the following day, and Carrara did not escape the
suspicion of having poisoned him.   These events happened
in the spring of 1404, while the duchess was still in
possession of Milan.   The only way of safety open to her
was to offer those towns to Venice as the price of her
assistance.   The Republic declared war against Francesco.
Vicenza of herself invited the Venetians to her aid, and
raised the standard of St Mark.   The Venetian armies
marched into the territory of Padua.   The flight and death
of the duchess made no difference in their operations :
Francesco was besieged in his capital ; Verona was forced
to surrender.   The war did not end till November 1405,
when Carrara and his sons were compelled to deliver themselves into the hands of Venice.   They were received at
first with a certain degree of respect, were placed at the
right and left hand of the doge, who temperately chided
them for their ingratitude.   But they were too powerful and
too much beloved by their subjects to be allowed to live.

On January 16, 1406, Francesco was strangled in prison after bravely defending himself against his murderers, and his two sons, not long afterwards, suffered the same fate. In this way the two great houses of Carrara, and della Scala came to an end. Their possessions fell into the hands of Venice, and the banner of St Mark floated over the walls of Treviso, Feltre, Belluno, Verona, Vicenza, and Padua. It is very doubtful if this large extension of power on the mainland was of any lasting value to the Republic.

From about the first decade of the fifteenth century the history of Italy takes a new departure. From being a history of separate towns, it becomes a history of small states. Venice laid the foundation of a state upon the mainland ; the duchy of Visconti, temporarily overthrown, was afterwards consolidated anew by the conquest of Pisa in 1406; Florence extinguished the liberty of that Republic, and made the modern Tuscany possible. A king of Naples arose who quelled the dissensions of his realms, and made Naples once more an important factor in the fortunes of the peninsula. His career is so intimately bound up with the history of the papal schism that it will be better now to give an account of both. We shall then have reached a point from which we may conveniently look back upon the past and forward to the future.

Pope Urban VI., of the German obedience, died on October 15, 1389. He was succeeded by Pietro Tomacelli, a Neapolitan, who assumed the title of Boniface IX., a young man thirty years of age. He relieved the house of Durazzo from the ban which lay upon it, and Ladislaus, son of Charles Durazzo, was crowned by his vicar, king of Naples, being at that time a boy of fifteen. Clement VII., the pope of the French obedience, died on September 16, 1394. The University of Paris and the king of France did what they could to hinder the election of a successor, but the French cardinals were obstinate. It was for their advantage that the schism should continue, and their choice fell on Pietro da Luna, a Spaniard, who took the name of Benedict XIII. He pretended to be jealous for the unity of the church, and made preparations for a conference with Boniface and his supporters, but it is doubtful whether he really wished for anything of the kind. Boniface was supported by Ladislaus, and through his assistance he acquired in 1398 the *dominium* or sovereignty of Rome, being the first pope who had ever been recognised as temporal lord of the Eternal City. This was another step towards the substitution of small states for independent towns in Italy which has been already mentioned. The last act of Boniface was the war with the Visconti, by which he gained possession of Bologna and Perugia. He died lord of the states of the church on October 1, 1404. He was a strong man, and a born ruler, the second founder of the temporal power of the popes.

After the death of Boniface the people of Rome rose in tumult. The cardinals came together in conclave, paralyzed with fear. They signed an undertaking that if any of them were elected pope he would abdicate when the interests of the church seemed to require it, and then chose as pope another Neapolitan, Cosimo de' Migliorati, who took the title of Innocent VII. His pontificate, which lasted two years, was very stormy. Ladislaus, who had been to Zara to receive the crown of Hungary, hurried to Rome as soon as he heard of the death of Boniface, and reached it on October 19. He made a kind of agreement between the Roman people and the new pontiff, which restored to them something of the self-government which they had lost. But this concord only lasted a short time. The impetuous nephews of the pope massacred the representatives of the people as they sought to approach the Holy Father; the town rose in tumult, the pope was obliged to fly, and took refuge at Perugia. The Romans were not more contented with the government of Ladislaus than they had been with that of Boniface, they willingly resigned their independence to the pope's vicar. Innocent VII. consented reluctantly to receive their overtures, and returned to his palace, where, after making peace with Ladislaus, he died quietly on November 6, 1406.

The fourteen Roman cardinals hesitated at first as to whether they should nominate a successor to Innocent. Self-interest, however, prevailed, and they chose a Venetian, Angelo Correr, having first impressed upon him that he was to do all in his power to put an end to the schism. He took the name of Gregory XII. He was an old man over seventy years of age. He agreed to resign his dignity if the Spanish pope, Pietro da Luna, would do the same. The condition of the Church was indeed most disastrous; all good men desired that the schism should come to an end. The Rector of the University of Paris took the lead in urging a reconciliation, and a meeting of the two popes was arranged at Savona. Ladislaus naturally wished to prevent the possible victory of a pope attached to the interests of France, but Correr set out for the rendezvous. Ladislaus took advantage of his absence to lay siege to Rome, and soon becoming master of it, made his triumphal entry on April 25, 1408. He was now an incarnation of hope to the weary Italians; he received ambassadors from various parts of the peninsula, and already began to look forward to becoming king of Italy, and perhaps emperor. If Ladislaus had not succeeded in conquering Rome it is possible that Benedict XIII. might have seized it by a *coup de main*, and seated himself on the vacant pontifical throne. As it was, the occupation of Rome by a foreign power, gave an excuse to both powers to decline the union. Benedict remained at Porte Venere, Gregory at Siena and Lucca. At last the patience of the Church was exhausted. The cardinals on both sides left their masters and determined to hold a council at Pisa, which met on March 25, 1409, Ladislaus in vain trying to hinder it. On June 5, the council of Pisa deposed both popes, as heretics and schismatics, and elected Pietro Filargo, an old man of seventy, native of Candia, as pope. He took the name of Alexander V. He was a Venetian by origin, and a Greek by birth, there having been no Greek pope since John VII. in the year 705. The catholic world now possessed three popes— Benedict XII., recognised by Arragon and Scotland; Gregory XII., obeyed by Naples, Hungary, Bavaria, and the emperor; and Alexander V., the pope of the Council. But Alexander soon received powerful support. Lewis of Anjou, the pretender to the crown of Naples, hastened to Pisa, the Florentines and the Viennese joined in the league which was formed against Ladislaus. Balthazar Cossa, the papal legate, more powerful than the pope himself, put himself at the head of the enterprise; and the military command was entrusted to Malatesta, who had, as lieutenant under him, Sforza d' Attendolo, and Braccio de Montone, two famous *condottieri*, who were soon to fill Italy with their quarrels. The enterprise was successful; town after town surrendered, and in January 1410 Rome did homage to her new master. We now stand on the verge of a new era. The Council of Pisa had opened the eyes of the Church, and shewn that the power it possessed was not concentrated in the papal office. The Council of Constance was the immediate successor of the Council of Pisa, and the Council of Constance points significantly to the German reformation.

POPES (1250 A.D.—1409 A.D.).

INNOCENT IV. (Fiesco). June 24, 1243—December 7, 1254.
ALEXANDER IV. (da Segni). December 27, 1254—May 25, 1261.
URBAN IV. (de Court Palais). August 29, 1261—October 2, 1264.
CLEMENT IV. (Fulcodi). February 6, 1265—November 29, 1268.
GREGORY X. (Visconti). October 1, 1271—January 10, 1276.
INNOCENT V. February 21—June 22, 1276.
HADRIAN V. (Fiesco). July 12—August 17, 1276.
JOHN XX. September 13, 1276—May 10, 1277.
NICOLAS III. (Orsini). November 25, 1277—August 22, 1280.
MARTIN IV. (de Brie). February 22, 1281—March 28, 1285.
NICOLAS IV. (Masci). February 15, 1288—April 4, 1292.
CELESTINE IV. (da Morrone). July 5—December 13, 1294.
BONIFACE VIII. (Gaetani). December 24, 1294—October 11, 1303.
BENEDICT XI. (Bocasino). October 23, 1303—July 7, 1304.
CLEMENT V. (de Goth). June 5, 1305—April 20, 1314.

IN AVIGNON.

JOHN XXI. (de Vese). August 7, 1316—December 3, 1334.
BENEDICT XII. (Fournier). December 20, 1334—April 25, 1342.
CLEMENT VI. (de Beaufort). May 7, 1342—December 6, 1352.
INNOCENT VI. (d'Albret). December 18, 1352—September 12, 1362.
URBAN V. (de Grisac). September 28, 1362—December 19, 1370.
GREGORY XI. (de Beaufort). December 30, 1370—March 27, 1378.
CLEMENT VII. (Roger, Comte de Genevois). September 21, 1378—
    September 16, 1394.
BENEDICT XIII. (da Luna). September 28, 1394—July 26, 1417.

IN ROME.

URBAN VI. (Prignani). April 6, 1378—October 15, 1389.
BONIFACE IX. (Tomaselli). November 2, 1389—October 1, 1404.
INNOCENT VII. (de' Meliorati). October 17, 1404—November 6, 1406.
GREGORY XII. (Corrario). November 30, 1406—June 5, 1409.
ALEXANDER V. (Filargi). June 26, 1409—May 3, 1410.

DOGES OF VENICE (1249—1413).

MARINO MOROSINI.   1249—1252.

RAINERIO ZENO.   1252—1268.

LORENZO TIEPOLI.   1268—1275.

JACOPO CONTARINI.   1275—1279.

GIOVANNI DANDOLO.   1279—1289.

PIETRO GRADENIGO.   1289—1311.

MARINO GEORGIO.   1311—1312.

GIOVANNI SORANZO.   1312—1327.

FRANCESCO DANDOLO.   1328—1339.

BARTOLOMMEO GRADENIGO.   1339—1342.

ANDREA DANDOLO.   1343—1354.

MARINO FALIERO.   1354—1355.

GIOVANNI GRADENIGO.   1355—1356.

GIOVANNI DELFINO.   1356—1361.

LORENZO CELSI.   1361—1365.

MARCO CORNARO.   1365—1367.

ANDREA CONTARINI.   1367—1382.

MICHELE MOROSINI.   June 10—October 16, 1382.

ANTON VENIERI.   1282—1400.

MICHELE STENO.   1400—1413.

HOUSE OF LUXEMBURG.

HENRY (III.),
Duke of Luxemburg, 1288—1313.
King of Germany (VII.), 1308.
Emperor (VII.), 1312.

JOHN. Duke, 1313—1346.
King of Bohemia, 1310.
Married ELIZABETH of Bohemia.

CHARLES IV.
1346—1353 King of Germany
and Bohemia.
Emperor, 1355.

WENCESLAUS I.,
1353—1383.

WENCESLAUS I.,
1383—1388.
King of Germany, 1376.
King of Bohemia, 1378—1419.

SIGISMUND,
King of Bohemia, 1419—1437.
King of Hungary, 1387.
King of Germany, 1419.
Emperor, 1433.

KINGS OF BOHEMIA.

WENCESLAUS I., 1230—1253.

OTTOCAR II., 1253—1278.
Duke of Austria,   1251.
Duke of Styria,   1260.
Duke of Carinthia, 1269.
Married MARGARET of
Austria, 1252.

RUDOLPH
of Austria
King of Bohemia,
October 15, 1306
—July 4, 1307.

= ELIZABETH =
of Poland

WENCESLAUS II.,
1278—1305.
King of Poland, 1300—1305.

WENCESLAUS III.,
1305—1306.
King of Hungary,
1301—1305.

ANNE = HENRY,
Duke of Carinthia.
King of Bohemia,
1307—1310.

ELIZABETH = JOHN
of Luxemburg.
King of Bohemia,
1310—1346.

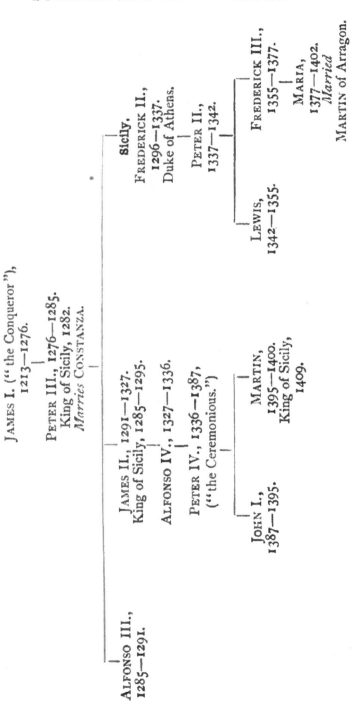

KINGS OF ARRAGON.

JAMES I. (" the Conqueror "),
1213—1276.

PETER III., 1276—1285.
King of Sicily, 1282.
Marries CONSTANZA.

ALFONSO III.,
1285—1291.

JAMES II., 1291—1327.
King of Sicily, 1285—1295.

ALFONSO IV., 1327—1336.

PETER IV., 1336—1387,
("the Ceremonious.")

JOHN I.,
1387—1395.

MARTIN,
1395—1400.
King of Sicily,
1409.

Sicily.
FREDERICK II.,
1296—1337.
Duke of Athens.

PETER II.,
1337—1342.

LEWIS,
1342—1355.

FREDERICK III.,
1355—1377.

MARIA,
1377—1402.
Married
MARTIN of Arragon.

THE HOHENSTAUFFEN EMPERORS.

FREDERICK I. (Barbarossa).
  Duke of Swabia, 1147—1152.
  King of Germany, 1152—
  Emperor, June 18, 1155—June 20, 1190.

HENRY VI.
  Joint King, 1169.
  King,   1190.
  Emperor, April 14, 1191—September 28, 1197.
  Married CONSTANZA, heiress of Sicily.

FREDERICK II., *born* December 26, 1193.
  Joint King of Germany, 1195.
  King of Sicily,   1197.
  King of Germany,   1215.
  Emperor,   1220.
  King of Jerusalem,   1229.
  Deposed at Lyons,   1245.
  Died December 26,   1250.

HENRY VII.,
died 1242.

CONRAD IV.,
King of Germany, 1250—1254.
Married ELIZABETH of Bavaria.

CONRADIN,
Duke of Swabia
and King of Sicily,
1254—1268.

MARGARET.

ENZIO,
King of
Sardinia.

MANFRED,
King of Sicily,
1258—1266.

FREDERICK,
Prince of Antioch.

CONSTANZA,
Married PETER III.,
King of Arragon.

KINGS OF FRANCE (1250—1409).

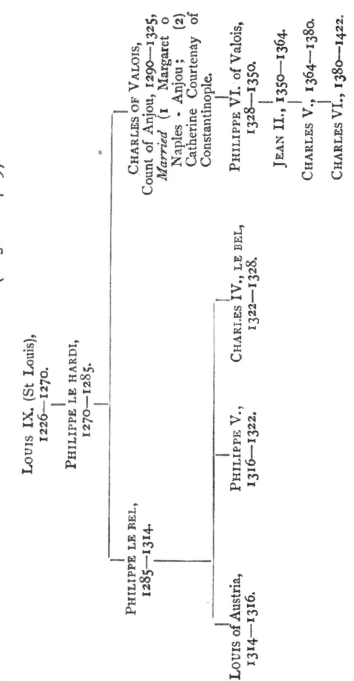

Louis IX. (St Louis),
1226—1270.

Philippe le Hardi,
1270—1285.

Philippe le Bel,
1285—1314.

Charles of Valois,
Count of Anjou, 1290—1325,
Married (1 Margaret o
Naples - Anjou; (2)
Catherine Courtenay of
Constantinople.

Charles IV., Le Bel,
1322—1328.

Philippe V.,
1316—1322.

Louis of Austria,
1314—1316.

Philippe VI. of Valois,
1328—1350.

Jean II., 1350—1364.

Charles V., 1364—1380.

Charles VI., 1380—1422.

ANGEVIN KINGS OF NAPLES.

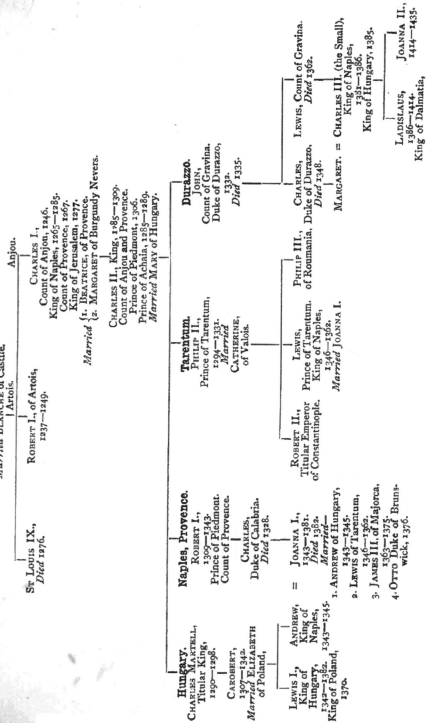

LOUIS VIII., King of France, *died* 1226.
Married BLANCHE of Castile.

St LOUIS IX., *Died* 1276.

ROBERT I., of Artois, 1237—1249.

Artois.

Anjou.

CHARLES I., 1246.
Count of Anjou, 1265—1285.
King of Naples, 1265—1285.
Count of Provence, 1267.
King of Jerusalem, 1277.
Married {1. BEATRICE, of Provence.
{2. MARGARET of Burgundy Nevers.

CHARLES II., King, 1285—1309.
Count of Anjou and Provence.
Prince of Piedmont, 1306.
Prince of Achaia, 1285—1289.
Married MARY of Hungary.

Hungary.
CHARLES MARTELL, Titular King, 1290—1298.

CAROBERT, 1307—1342.
Married ELIZABETH of Poland,

LEWIS I., King of Hungary, 1342—1382.
King of Poland, 1370.

ANDREW, King of Naples, 1343—1345.

Naples, Provence.
ROBERT I., 1309—1343.
Prince of Piedmont.
Count of Provence.

CHARLES, Duke of Calabria. *Died* 1328.

JOANNA I., 1343—1381.
Died 1382.
Married—
1. ANDREW of Hungary, 1343—1345.
2. LEWIS of Tarentum, 1346—1362.
3. JAMES III., of Majorca, 1363—1375.
4. OTTO Duke of Brunswick, 1376.

=

Tarentum.
PHILIP II., Prince of Tarentum, 1294—1331.
Married CATHERINE, of Valois.

ROBERT II., Titular Emperor of Constantinople.

LEWIS, Prince of Tarentum. King of Naples, 1346—1362.
Married JOANNA I.

PHILIP III., of Roumania, of Durazzo. *Died* 1348.

Durazzo.
JOHN, Count of Gravina. Duke of Durazzo, 1332. *Died* 1335.

CHARLES, Duke of Durazzo, *Died* 1348.

MARGARET. = CHARLES III. (the Small), King of Naples, 1381—1386. King of Hungary, 1385.

LEWIS, Count of Gravina. *Died* 1362.

LADISLAUS, 1386—1414. King of Dalmatia, 1403—1409.

JOANNA II., 1414—1435.

DUKES OF MILAN.

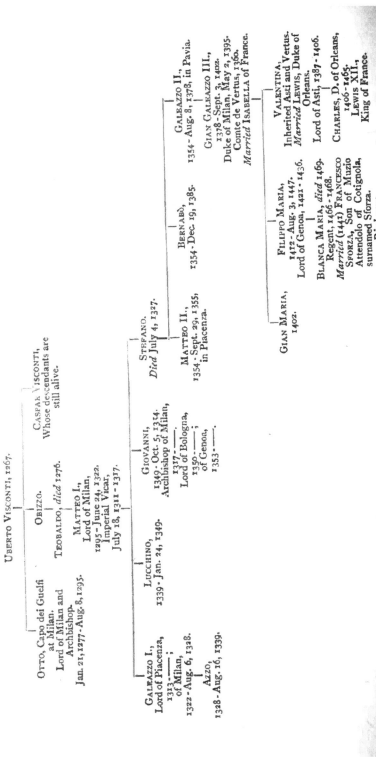

UBERTO VISCONTI, 1267.

OTTO, Capo dei Guelfi at Milan. Lord of Milan and Archbishop. Jan. 21, 1277 - Aug. 8, 1295.

OBIZZO. TEOBALDO, *died* 1276.

CASPAR VISCONTI, Whose descendants are still alive.

MATTEO I., Lord of Milan, 1295 - June 24, 1322. Imperial Vicar, July 18, 1311 - 1317.

GALEAZZO I., Lord of Piacenza, 1313 - ——; of Milan, 1322 - Aug. 6, 1328.

AZZO, 1328 - Aug. 16, 1339.

LUCCHINO, 1339 - Jan. 24, 1349.

GIOVANNI, 1349 - Oct. 5, 1354. Archbishop of Milan, 1317 - Lord of Bologna, 1350 - ——; of Genoa, 1353 - ——.

STEFANO. *Died* July 4, 1327.

MATTEO II., 1354 - Sept. 29, 1355, in Piacenza.

BERNABÒ, 1354 - Dec. 19, 1385.

GALEAZZO II., 1354 - Aug. 8, 1378, in Pavia.

GIAN GALEAZZO III., 1378 - Sept. 3, 1402. Duke of Milan, May 2, 1395. Conte de Vertus, 1360. *Married* ISABELLA of France.

GIAN MARIA, 1402.

FILIPPO MARIA, 1412 - Aug. 3, 1447. Lord of Genoa, 1421 - 1436.

BLANCA MARIA, *died* 1469. Regent, 1466 - 1468. *Married* (1441) FRANCESCO SFORZA, Son of Muzio Attendolo of Cotignola, surnamed Sforza. *Died* 1424.

VALENTINA, Inherited Asti and Vertus. *Married* LEWIS, Duke of Orleans. Lord of Asti, 1387 - 1406.

CHARLES, D. of Orleans, 1406 - 1465. LEWIS XII., King of France.

THE SCALIGERS (Della Scala).

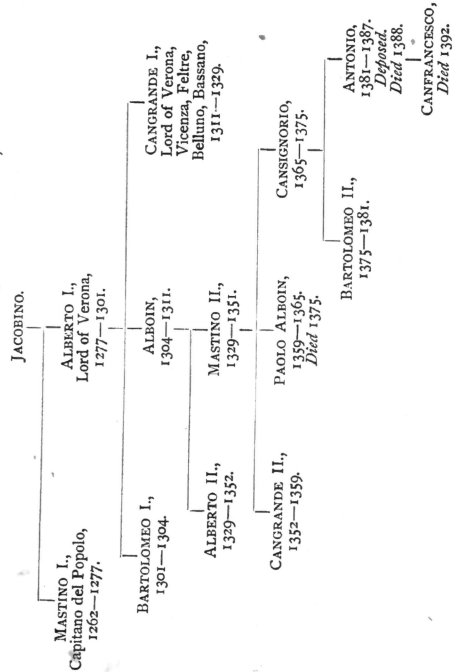

Jacobino.

Mastino I., Capitano del Popolo, 1262—1277.

Alberto I., Lord of Verona, 1277—1301.

Bartolomeo I., 1301—1304.

Cangrande I., Lord of Verona, Vicenza, Feltre, Belluno, Bassano, 1311—1329.

Alboin, 1304—1311.

Alberto II., 1329—1352.

Mastino II., 1329—1351.

Cangrande II., 1352—1359.

Paolo Alboin, 1359—1365. Died 1375.

Cansignorio, 1365—1375.

Bartolomeo II., 1375—1381.

Antonio, 1381—1387. Deposed. Died 1388.

Canfrancesco, Died 1392.

INDEX.

TURNBULL AND SPEARS, PRINTERS, EDINBURGH.

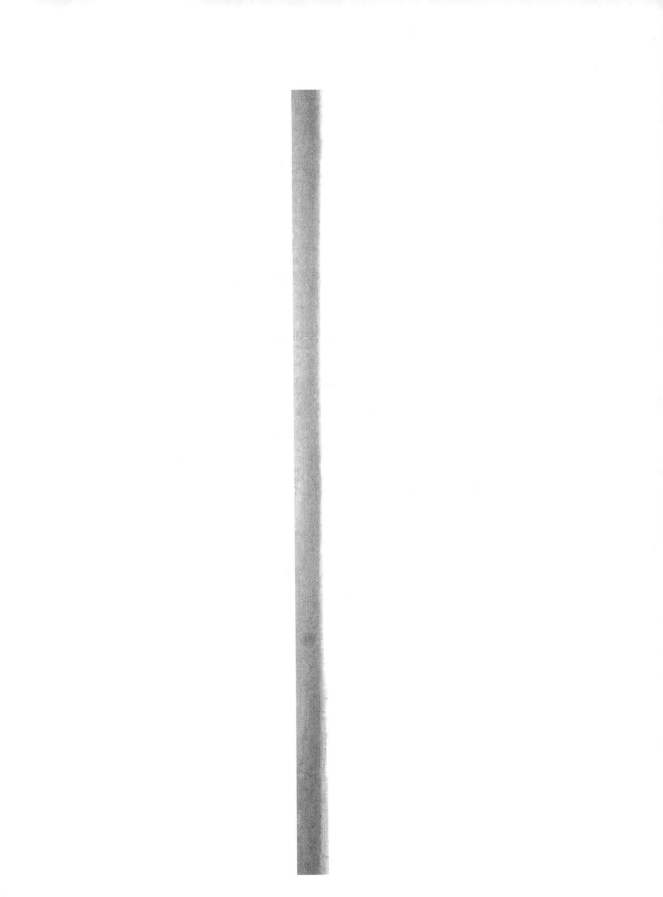

BY THE SAME AUTHOR

A LIST OF EDUCATIONAL WORKS PUBLISHED BY METHUEN AND COMPANY PUBLISHERS : LONDON 36 ESSEX STREET W.C.

CONTENTS

MESSRS. METHUEN WILL BE GLAD TO SEND THEIR COMPLETE CATALOGUE OR PROSPECTUSES OF ANY OF THEIR SERIES TO ANY ADDRESS, POST FREE, ON APPLICATION

1903

NOTE

MESSRS. METHUEN will be happy to receive applications for Specimen Copies of any of their School Books from *bonâ-fide* Teachers. Specimen Copies of many of their School Books are supplied gratis, but a charge must be made in all cases for books marked with an asterisk in this List. Specimen Copies of Keys are not given.

A copy of any book in this List can be seen at Messrs. Methuen's offices, 36 Essex Street, Strand, W.C., and most of them may be consulted at the Library of The Teachers' Guild, 74 Gower Street, W.C., and at the Library of the College of Preceptors, Bloomsbury Square, W.C.

A copy of each of Messrs. Methuen's Educational Books is sent to the Education Department Libraries in the Colonies.

MESSRS. METHUEN'S
EDUCATIONAL LIST

———— ✣ ————

Classical

*The Nicomachean Ethics of Aristotle. Edited, with an Introduction and Notes, by JOHN BURNET, M.A., Professor of Greek at St. Andrews. Demy 8vo, 15s. net.

This edition contains parallel passages from the Eudemian Ethics, printed under the text, and there is a full commentary, the main object of which is to interpret difficulties in the light of Aristotle's own rules.

*The Captivi of Plautus. Edited, with an Introduction, Textual Notes, and a Commentary, by W. M. LINDSAY, Fellow of Jesus College, Oxford. Demy 8vo, 10s. 6d. net.

For this edition all the important MSS. have been re-collated. An Appendix deals with the accentual element in early Latin verse. The Commentary is very full.

*Plauti Bacchides. Edited, with Introduction, Commentary, and Critical Notes, by J. M'COSH, M.A. Fcap. 4to, 12s. 6d.

Taciti Agricola. With Introduction, Notes, Map, etc. By R. F. DAVIS, M.A., late Assistant Master at Weymouth College. Crown 8vo, 2s.

Taciti Germania. By the same Editor. Crown 8vo, 2s.

Herodotus: Easy Selections. With Vocabulary. By A. C. LIDDELL, M.A., of Westminster School. Fcap. 8vo, 1s. 6d.

Demosthenes against Conon and Callicles. Edited, with Notes and Vocabulary, by F. D. SWIFT, M.A. Fcap. 8vo, 2s.

Selections from the Odyssey. By E. D. STONE, M.A., late Assistant Master at Eton. Fcap. 8vo, 1s. 6d.

Plautus: The Captivi. Adapted for Lower Forms by J. H. FREESE, M.A., late Fellow of St. John's, Cambridge. 1s. 6d.

*** A Greek Anthology.** Selected by E. C. MARCHANT, M.A., Fellow of Peterhouse, Cambridge. Crown 8vo, 3s. 6d.

*** New Testament Greek.** A Course for Beginners. By G RODWELL, B.A. With a Preface by WALTER LOCK, D.D., Warden of Keble College. Fcap. 8vo, 3s. 6d.

Aims at helping those many grown-up people, who not having learnt Greek at school, desire to learn the language of the Gospels.

Exercises in Latin Accidence. By S. E. WINBOLT, Assistant Master in Christ's Hospital. Crown 8vo, 1s. 6d.

An elementary book for Lower Forms to accompany the shorter Latin Primer.

*** Notes on Greek and Latin Syntax.** By G. BUCKLAND GREEN, M.A., Assistant Master at Edinburgh Academy, late Fellow of St. John's College, Oxon. Crown 8vo, 3s. 6d.

Notes and explanations on the chief difficulties of Greek and Latin syntax, with numerous passages for exercise, for the higher forms of schools and the universities.

Passages for Unseen Translation. By E. C. MARCHANT, M.A., Fellow of Peterhouse, Cambridge; and A. M. COOK, M.A., Assistant Master at St. Paul's School. Second Edition. Cr. 8vo, 3s. 6d.

Two hundred Latin and two hundred Greek passages, arranged in order of increasing difficulty. Has been carefully compiled to meet the wants of V. and VI. form boys at the public schools, and is also well adapted for the use of honourmen at the universities. Prose and verse alternate throughout.

" We know no book of this class better fitted for use in the higher forms of schools.'
—*Guardian.*

Scriptorum Classicorum Bibliotheca Oxoniensis

OXFORD CLASSICAL TEXTS, 1900

*** Thucydidis Historiae.** Libri I.–IV. By H. STUART JONES. Crown 8vo, paper covers, 3s. ; limp cloth, 3s. 6d.

*** Platonis Opera.** Tom. I. (Tetralogiae I.–II.). By J. BURNET. Crown 8vo, paper covers, 5s. ; limp cloth, 6s.

*** Lvcreti Cari de Rervm Natvra.** By C. BAILEY. Crown 8vo, paper covers, 2s. 6d. ; limp cloth, 3s.

*** Cornelii Taciti Opera Minora.** By H. FURNEAUX. Crown 8vo, paper covers, 1s. 6d. ; limp cloth, 2s.

*** Aeschyli Tragoediae cum Fragmentis.** By A. SIDGWICK. Crown 8vo, paper covers, 3s. ; limp cloth, 3s. 6d.

* **Apollonii Rhodii Argonautica.** By R. C. SEATON. Crown 8vo, paper covers, 2s. 6d. ; limp cloth, 3s.

* **Aristophanis Comoediae.** Tom. I. By F. W. HALL and W. M. GELDART. Crown 8vo, paper covers, 3s. ; limp cloth, 3s. 6d.

* **Xenophontis Opera.** Tom. I. (Historia Graeca). By E. C. MARCHANT. Crown 8vo, paper covers, 2s. 6d. ; limp cloth, 3s.

* **Caesaris Commentarii de Bello Gallico.** By R. L. A. DU PONTET. Crown 8vo, paper covers, 2s. ; limp cloth, 2s. 6d.

* **Vergili Opera.** By F. A. HIRTZEL. Crown 8vo, paper covers, 3s. ; limp cloth, 3s. 6d.

Classical Translations

EDITED BY H. F. FOX, M.A.,
FELLOW AND TUTOR OF BRASENOSE COLLEGE, OXFORD

Messrs. METHUEN are issuing a New Series of Translations from the Greek and Latin Classics. They have enlisted the services of some of the best Oxford and Cambridge Scholars, and it is their intention that the Series shall be distinguished by literary excellence, as well as by scholarly accuracy.

Crown 8vo. Finely printed.

* **Cicero. De Oratore I.** Translated by E. N. P. MOOR, M.A., late Assistant Master at Clifton. 3s. 6d.

* **Aeschylus — Agamemnon, Chöephoroe, Eumenides.** Translated by LEWIS CAMPBELL, LL.D. 5s.

* **Lucian — Six Dialogues** (Nigrinus, Icaro-Menippus, The Cock, The Ship, The Parasite, The Lover of Falsehood). Translated by S. T. IRWIN, M.A., Assistant Master at Clifton. 3s. 6d.

* **Sophocles—Electra and Ajax.** Translated by E. D. A. MORSHEAD, M.A., Assistant Master at Winchester. 2s. 6d.

* **Tacitus—Agricola and Germania.** Translated by R. B. TOWNSHEND, late Scholar of Trinity College, Cambridge. 2s. 6d.

* **Cicero—Select Orations** (Pro Milone, Pro Murena, Philippic II., In Catilinam). Translated by H. E. D. BLAKISTON, M.A., Fellow and Tutor of Trinity College, Oxford. 5s.

* **Cicero—De Natura Deorum.** Translated by F. BROOKS, M.A., late Scholar of Balliol College, Oxford. 3s. 6d.

* **Horace : The Odes and Epodes.** Translated by A. GODLEY, M.A., Fellow of Magdalen College, Oxford. 2s.

* **Cicero de Officiis.** Translated by G. B. GARDINER, M.A. Crown 8vo, 2s. 6d.

Uniform with the above.

* **The Frogs of Aristophanes.** Translated by E. W. HUNTINGFORD, M.A., Professor of Classics in Trinity College, Toronto. Crown 8vo, 2s. 6d.

* **Demosthenes** : The Olynthiacs and Philippics. Translated on a new principle by OTHO HOLLAND. Crown 8vo, 2s. 6d.

WORKS BY A. M. M. STEDMAN, M.A.

Initia Latina : Easy Lessons on Elementary Accidence. Sixth Edition. Fcap. 8vo, 1s.

First Latin Lessons. Sixth Edition. Crown 8vo, 2s.

First Latin Reader. With Notes adapted to the Shorter Latin Primer, and Vocabulary. Sixth Edition. 18mo, 1s. 6d.

Easy Selections from Caesar. Part I. The Helvetian War. With Notes and Vocabulary. Illustrated. Second Edition. 18mo, 1s.

Easy Selections from Livy. Part I. The Kings of Rome. With Notes and Vocabulary. Illustrated. Second Edition. 18mo, 1s. 6d.

Easy Latin Passages for Unseen Translation. Eighth Edition. Fcap. 8vo, 1s. 6d.

Exempla Latina : First Exercises in Latin Accidence. With Vocabulary. Crown 8vo, 1s.

Easy Latin Exercises on the Syntax of the Shorter and Revised Latin Primer. With Vocabulary. Ninth Edition. Crown 8vo, 1s. 6d. Issued with the consent of Dr. KENNEDY. Key, 3s. net. Original Edition. 2s. 6d.

The Latin Compound Sentence : Rules and Exercises. Second Edition. Crown 8vo, 1s. 6d. ; with Vocabulary, 2s.

Notanda Quaedam : Miscellaneous Latin Exercises on Common Rules and Idioms. Fourth Edition. Fcap. 8vo, 1s. 6d. ; with Vocabulary, 2s. Key, 2s. net.

Latin Vocabularies for Repetition : Arranged according to Subjects. Eleventh Edition. Fcap. 8vo, 1s. 6d.

A Vocabulary of Latin Idioms and Phrases. Second Edition. 18mo, 1s.

Steps to Greek. Second Edition, Revised. 18mo, 1s.

A Shorter Greek Primer. Crown 8vo, 1s. 6d.

Easy Greek Passages for Unseen Translation. Third Edition. Fcap. 8vo, 1s. 6d.

Easy Greek Exercises on Elementary Syntax. By C. G. Botting, B.A., Assistant Master at St. Paul's School. Crown 8vo, 2s.

Greek Vocabularies for Repetition: Arranged according to Subjects. Third Edition. Fcap. 8vo, 1s. 6d.

Greek Testament Selections. For the Use of Schools. Third Edition. With Introduction, Notes, and Vocabulary. Fcap. 8vo, 2s. 6d.

Steps to French. Sixth Edition. 18mo, 8d.

First French Lessons. Sixth Edition. Crown 8vo, 1s.

Easy French Passages for Unseen Translation. Fifth Edition. Fcap. 8vo, 1s. 6d.

Easy French Exercises on Elementary Syntax. With Vocabulary. Second Edition. Crown 8vo, 2s. 6d. **Key,** 3s. net.

French Vocabularies for Repetition: Arranged according to Subjects. Tenth Edition. Fcap. 8vo, 1s.

German Vocabularies for Repetition: Arranged according to Subjects. By Sophie Wright, late Scholar of Bedford College, London. Fcap. 8vo, 1s. 6d.

School Examination Series

Edited by A. M. M. STEDMAN, M.A.

Crown 8vo, 2s. 6d. each

This Series is intended for the use of teachers and students, to supply material for the former and practice for the latter. The papers are carefully graduated, cover the whole of the subject usually taught, and are intended to form part of the ordinary class work. They may be used *vivâ voce*, or as a written examination. This Series is now in use in a large number of public and private schools, including Eton, Harrow, Winchester, Repton, Cheltenham, Sherborne, Haileybury, Manchester Grammar School, Merchant Taylors, etc.

*French Examination Papers in Miscellaneous Grammar and Idioms. By A. M. M. Stedman, M.A. Eleventh Edition.

    A Key, issued to Tutors and Private Students only, to be had on application to the Publishers. Fifth Edition. Crown 8vo, 6s. net.

*Latin Examination Papers in Miscellaneous Grammar and Idioms. By A. M. M. STEDMAN, M.A. Eleventh Edition. Key (Fourth Edition), issued as above, 6s. net.

* Greek Examination Papers in Miscellaneous Grammar and Idioms. By A. M. M. STEDMAN, M.A. Sixth Edition. Key (Second Edition), issued as above, 6s. net.

* German Examination Papers in Miscellaneous Grammar and Idioms. By R. J. MORICH, late Assistant Master at Clifton. Sixth Edition. Key (Second Edition), issued as above, 6s. net.

* History and Geography Examination Papers. By C. H. SPENCE, M.A., Clifton College. Second Edition.

* Physics Examination Papers. By R. E. STEEL, M.A., F.C.S., Principal, Technical College, Northampton. Papers on Sound, Light, Heat, Magnetism, Electricity.

* General Knowledge Examination Papers. By A. M. M. STEDMAN, M.A. Fourth Edition. Key (Second Edition), issued as above, 7s. net.

* Examination Papers in Book-keeping. With Preliminary Exercises. Compiled and Arranged by J. T. MEDHURST, F.S.Accts. and Auditors, and Lecturer at City of London College. Seventh Edition. 3s. Key, 2s. 6d. net.

* English Literature Examination Papers. Chiefly Collected from College Papers set at Cambridge. With an Introduction on the Study of English. By W. W. SKEAT, Litt.D., LL.D., Professor of Anglo-Saxon at Cambridge University. Third Edition, Revised.

* Arithmetic Examination Papers. By C. PENDLEBURY, M.A., Senior Mathematical Master, St. Paul's School. Fifth Edition. With answers. Key, 5s. net.

* Trigonometry Examination Papers. By G. H. WARD, M.A., late Assistant Master at St. Paul's School. Fourth Edition. Key, 5s. net.

* Examination Papers on the Constitutional and General History of England. By J. TAIT PLOWDEN-WARDLAW, M.A., King's College, Cambridge.

Junior Examination Series

EDITED BY A. M. M. STEDMAN, M.A.

Fcap. 8vo, 1s. each

This Series is intended to lead up to the School Examination Series and for candidates preparing for the Oxford and Cambridge Junior Local Examinations. Each volume contains 720 carefully graduated *original* questions divided into papers of ten questions each. The papers are so arranged that each may be marked with the same maximum number of marks. By this means the progress of the pupil can be easily ascertained.

* **Junior French Examination Papers in Miscellaneous Grammar and Idioms.** By F. JACOB, M.A., Modern Language Master at Cheltenham College.

* **Junior Latin Examination Papers in Miscellaneous Grammar and Idioms.** By C. G. BOTTING, B.A., Assistant Master at St. Paul's School.

* **Junior English Examination Papers.** By W. WILLIAMSON, B.A., Headmaster, West Kent Grammar School, Brockley.

* **Junior Arithmetic Examination Papers.** By W. S. BEARD, Headmaster, The Modern School, Fareham. With answers. Contains 900 questions arranged in papers to ten each.

* **Junior Algebra Examination Papers.** By S. W. FINN, M.A., Headmaster, Sandbach School. With answers.

Methuen's Commercial Series

EDITED BY H. DE B. GIBBINS, LITT.D., M.A.

Crown 8vo.

This Series is intended to assist students and young men preparing for a commercial career, by supplying useful handbooks of a practical character, dealing with those subjects which are absolutely essential in business life.

British Commerce and Colonies from Elizabeth to Victoria. By H. DE B. GIBBINS, Litt.D., M.A., Author of "The Industrial History of England," etc. Third Edition. 2s.

A Manual of French Commercial Correspondence. By S. E. BALLY, Modern Language Master at the Manchester Grammar School. With Vocabulary. Third Edition. 2s.

A Manual of German Commercial Correspondence. By S. E. BALLY. With Vocabulary. 2s. 6d.

A German Commercial Reader. By S. E. BALLY. With Vocabulary. 2s.

A French Commercial Reader. By S. E. BALLY. With Vocabulary. Second Edition. 2s.

A Commercial Geography of the British Empire. With special reference to Trade Routes, Manufacturing Districts, etc. By L. W. LYDE, M.A., Grammar School, Bolton. Third Edition. 2s.

A Commercial Geography of Foreign Nations. By F. C. BOON, B.A. Crown 8vo, 2s.

*** Commercial Examination Papers.** By H. DE B. GIBBINS, Litt.D. Papers on Commercial Geography and History, French and German Correspondence, Book-keeping, and Office Work. 1s. 6d.

The Economics of Commerce. By H. DE B. GIBBINS, Litt.D., M.A. 1s. 6d.

A Primer of Business. By S. JACKSON, M.A. Third Edition. 1s. 6d.

Commercial Arithmetic. By F. G. TAYLOR, M.A. Third Edition. 1s. 6d.

Précis Writing and Office Correspondence. By E. E. WHITFIELD, M.A. 2s.

The Principles of Book-keeping by Double Entry. By J. E. B. M'ALLEN, M.A. 2s.

Commercial Law. By W. DOUGLAS EDWARDS, LL.B. 2s.

*** A Guide to Professions and Business.** By HENRY JONES. 1s. 6d.

*** Commercial Education in Theory and Practice.** By E. E. WHITFIELD, M.A. 5s.

Treats of the whole question of Commercial Education. Reliable information as to the work done by young clerks in modern business establishments is given, also hints as to the bearing of school work on such duties. A number of examination papers and lists of books are included.

Technology.

*** Ornamental Design for Woven Fabrics.** By C. STEPHEN-SON, of the Technical College, Bradford; and F. SUDDARDS, of the Yorkshire College, Leeds. With 65 full-page Plates. Second Edition. Demy 8vo, 7s. 6d.

*** An Introduction to the Study of Textile Design.** By A. F. BARKER. Illustrated. Demy 8vo.

† **The Construction of Large Induction Coils.** By A. T. HARE, M.A. With numerous Diagrams. Demy 8vo, 6s.

† **Lace-Making in the Midlands, Past and Present.** By C. C. CHANNER and M. E. ROBERTS. Illustrated. Cr. 8vo, 2s. 6d.

† *Specimen copies not given.*

Text-Books of Technology.

EDITED BY W. GARNETT, D.C.L., SECRETARY OF THE TECHNICAL EDUCATION BOARD OF THE LONDON COUNTY COUNCIL; AND PROFESSOR J. WERTHEIMER, B.Sc., F.I.C., PRINCIPAL OF THE MERCHANT VENTURERS' TECHNICAL COLLEGE, BRISTOL.

Messrs. METHUEN are issuing a series of elementary books under the above title. They are specially adapted to the needs of Technical Schools and Colleges, and fulfil the requirements of students preparing for the examinations of the City and Guilds of London Institute.

Carpentry and Joinery. By F. C. WEBBER. With 176 Illustrations. Second Edition. Crown 8vo, 3s. 6d.

The drawings are intended to serve not only as illustrations, but also as examples for reproduction by the student.

"An admirable elementary text-book on the subject."—*Builder.*

Practical Mechanics. By SIDNEY H. WELLS. With 75 Illustrations and Diagrams. Second Edition. Crown 8vo, 3s. 6d.

Contains all that is necessary for the London Matriculation Examination and the Elementary course in Applied Mechanics of the Science and Art Department.

Practical Physics. By H. STROUD, D.Sc., M.A., Professor of Physics in the Durham College of Science, Newcastle-on-Tyne. With 115 Diagrams. Crown 8vo, 3s. 6d.

An introduction to the standard works on Practical Physics.

Arithmetic and Mensuration for the Workshop and Technical School. By C. T. MILLS, M.I.M.E., Principal of the Borough Polytechnic College. With Diagrams. Crown 8vo.

Practical Chemistry. By W. FRENCH, M.A., Principal of the Storey Institute, Lancaster. Part I. With 57 Diagrams. Crown 8vo, 1s. 6d.

Based on the scheme issued by the Education Department for Evening Continuation Schools and that of the Headmasters' Association. Suitable for Oxford and Cambridge Junior Locals. The teaching throughout is *inductive.*

How to make a Dress. By J. A. E. WOOD. Illustrated. Second Edition. Crown 8vo, 1s. 6d.

Millinery: Theoretical and Practical. By CLARE HILL. With numerous Diagrams. Crown 8vo, 2s.

Methuen's Science Primers.

EDITED BY PROFESSOR WERTHEIMER, B.Sc., F.I.C.

Messrs. METHUEN are issuing a series of elementary books dealing with the science subjects mentioned in the Directory of the Department of Science and Art. They will be suitable for use in Grammar Schools, Schools of Science, and Technical Institutions, and for candidates preparing for the examinations of the Department.

General Elementary Science. By J. T. DUNN, D.Sc., and V. A. MUNDELLA, M.A. With 114 Illustrations. Crown 8vo, 3s. 6d.

Specially intended for London Matriculation General Elementary Science Examination.

Science and Mathematics

The World of Science. Including Chemistry, Heat, Light, Sound, Magnetism, Electricity, Botany, Zoology, Physiology, Astronomy, and Geology. By R. ELLIOT STEEL, M.A., F.C.S. 147 Illustrations. Second Edition. Crown 8vo, 2s. 6d.

A Class-Book on Light. By R. E. STEEL. With numerous Illustrations. Crown 8vo, 2s. 6d.

A South African Arithmetic. By HENRY HILL, B.A., Headmaster, Boys' High School, Worcester, Cape Colony. Crown 8vo, 3s. 6d.

Test Cards in Euclid and Algebra. By D. S. CALDERWOOD, Headmaster of the Normal School, Edinburgh. In three packets of 40, with Answers. 1s. each ; or in three books, price 2d., 2d., and 3d.

The Metric System. By LEON DELBOS. Crown 8vo, 2s.
A theoretical and practical guide, for use in elementary schools and by the general reader. Contains a number of graduated problems with answers.

Agricultural Geology. By J. E. MARR, F.R.S. With numerous Illustrations. Crown 8vo.

Agricultural Zoology. By Dr. J. RITZEMA BOS. Translated by J. R. AINSWORTH DAVIS, M.A., Professor of Zoology, University College, Aberystwyth. With an Introduction by ELEANOR A. OMEROD, F.E.S. With 155 Illustrations. Second Edition, with full Index. Crown 8vo, 3s. 6d.

Dairy Bacteriology. A Short Manual for the Use of Students. By Dr. ED. VON FREUDENREICH. Translated by J. R. AINSWORTH DAVIS, M.A. Second Edition. Crown 8vo, 2s. 6d.

*Outlines of Biology. By P. CHALMERS MITCHELL, M.A. Illustrated. Second Edition. Crown 8vo, 6s.
A text-book designed to cover the new Schedule issued by the Royal College of Physicians and Surgeons.

Handbooks of Science

EDITED BY PROFESSORS J. B. FARMER, M.A., F.R.S., AND W. WATSON, B.SC., OF THE ROYAL COLLEGE OF SCIENCE, SOUTH KENSINGTON.

*The Scientific Study of Scenery. By J. E. MARR, M.A., F.R.S., Fellow of St. John's College, Cambridge. With numerous Illustrations and Diagrams. Crown 8vo, 6s.
An elementary treatise on geomorphology—the study of the earth's outward forms. It is for the use of students of physical geography and geology, and will also be highly interesting to the general reader.

The Principles of Magnetism and Electricity. An Elementary Text-Book. By P. L. GRAY, B.Sc., formerly Lecturer on Physics in Mason University College, Birmingham. With 181 Diagrams. Crown 8vo, 3s. 6d.
"A capital text-book. One which we can recommend with the utmost confidence."
—*Teachers' Review.*　　　　　　　"Perfectly reliable."—*Educational Times.*

English

The Rose Reader. By EDWARD ROSE. With numerous
Illustrations. Crown 8vo, 2s. 6d. And in Four Parts. Parts I. and II., 6d. each;
Part III., 8d. ; Part IV., 10d. Introduction for the Teacher separately, 6d.

A reader on a new and original plan. The distinctive feature of this book is the
entire avoidance of irregularly-spelt words until the pupil has thoroughly mastered the
principle of reading, and learned its enjoyment. The reading of connected sentences
begins from the first page, before the entire alphabet is introduced.

A Class Book of Easy Dictation and Spelling. By
W. WILLIAMSON, B.A. Fcap. 8vo, 1s.

A Short Story of English Literature. By EMMA S.
MELLOWS. Crown 8vo, 3s. 6d.

Ballads of the Brave. Poems of Chivalry, Enterprise, Courage,
and Constancy. Edited by F. LANGBRIDGE, M.A. Second Edition. 2s. 6d.

** **Tommy Smith's Animals.** By EDMUND SELOUS. With 8
Illustrations by G. W. ORD. Third Edition. Fcap. 8vo, 2s. 6d.

A reading-book for kindergarten and junior school libraries.

A Primer of the Bible. By W. H. BENNETT, M.A.
Crown 8vo, 2s. 6d.

A Primer of Tennyson. By W. M. DIXON, M.A. Second
Edition. Crown 8vo, 2s. 6d.

A Primer of Burns. By W. A. CRAIGIE. Crown 8vo, 2s. 6d.

A Primer of Wordsworth. By LAURIE MAGNUS, M.A.
Crown 8vo, 2s. 6d.

THE LITTLE LIBRARY

Pott 8vo. Each Vol. cloth, 1s. 6d. net ; leather, 2s. 6d. net.

Each, where it seems desirable, will contain an introduction, which will give (1) a
short biography of the author ; (2) a critical estimate of the book, and short notes at the
foot of the pages. Volumes of this series are in use in the Higher Forms of several Public
Schools, and in some of the Training Colleges.

** **A Little Book of English Prose.** Edited by Mrs. P. A.
BARNETT.

** **A Little Book of English Lyrics.**

** **A Little Book of Scottish Verse.** Edited by T. F. HEN-
DERSON.

** **The Early Poems of Alfred, Lord Tennyson.** Edited by
J. CHURTON COLLINS, M.A.

** **The Princess, and other Poems.** By ALFRED, LORD
TENNYSON. Edited by ELIZABETH WORDSWORTH.

** **Maud, and other Poems.** By ALFRED, LORD TENNYSON.
Edited by ELIZABETH WORDSWORTH.

** **In Memoriam.** By ALFRED, LORD TENNYSON. Edited by
H. C. BEECHING.

** **Selections from Wordsworth.** Edited by NOWELL C.
SMITH.

** **Eothen.** By A. W. KINGLAKE.

** **Elia, and the Last Essays of Elia.** By CHARLES LAMB.
Edited by E. V. LUCAS.

French and German

French Prose Composition. By R. R. N. BARON, M.A. With Vocabularies and Notes. Crown 8vo, 2s. 6d. **Key,** 3s. net. Suitable for use in Upper Forms and for Candidates for Army Examinations.

A Companion German Grammar. By H. DE B. GIBBINS Litt.D., M.A. Crown 8vo, 1s. 6d.

German Passages for Unseen Translation. By E. M'QUEEN GRAY. Crown 8vo, 2s. 6d.

See also pages 7-10.

History

The Makers of Europe. By E. M. WILMOT-BUXTON, Assistant Mistress, Brighton and Hove High School. Crown 8vo, 3s. 6d.
A text-book of European history suitable for the Middle Forms of Schools. The whole course is designed to fill about two years at the rate of two short lessons a week.

A Short History of Rome. By J. WELLS, M.A., Fellow and Tutor of Wadham College, Oxford. With 3 Maps. Fourth Edition. Crown 8vo, 3s. 6d.
"The schoolmasters who have felt the want of a fifth-form handbook of Roman history may congratulate themselves on persuading Mr. Wells to respond to it. His book is excellently planned and executed. Broken up into short paragraphs, with headings to arrest the attention, his manual does equal justice to the personal and the constitutional aspects of the story. Special credit is due to an author who, in the compilation of an elementary work of this kind, faces the difficulties of his subject with conscientious skill, neither ignoring them nor eluding them with a loose phrase, but striving to explain them in the simplest and briefest statements."—*Journal of Education.*

* **A Constitutional and Political History of Rome.** By T. M. TAYLOR, M.A., Fellow of Gonville and Caius College, Cambridge, Porson University Scholar, etc. etc. Crown 8vo, 7s. 6d.
An account of the origin and growth of the Roman institutions, and a discussion of the various political movements in Rome from the earliest times to the death of Augustus.

† **Battles of English History.** By H. B. GEORGE, M.A. With numerous Plans. Third Edition. Crown 8vo, 6s.

* **English Records.** A Companion to the History of England. By H. E. MALDEN, M.A. Crown 8vo, 3s. 6d.
A book which aims at concentrating information upon dates, genealogy, officials, constitutional documents, etc.; which is usually found scattered in different volumes.

General

The Students' Prayer Book. PART I. MORNING AND EVENING PRAYER AND LITANY. Edited by W. H. FLECKER, M.A., D.C.L., Headmaster of the Dean Close School, Cheltenham. Crown 8vo.

† **Educational Reform.** By FABIAN WARE, M.A. Cr. 8vo, 2s. 6d.

The Rights and Duties of the English Citizen. By H. E. MALDEN, M.A. 1s. 6d.

† *Specimens not given.*

University Extension Series

EDITED BY J. E. SYMES, M.A.,

PRINCIPAL OF UNIVERSITY COLLEGE, NOTTINGHAM

Crown 8vo. Price (with some exceptions) 2s. 6d

A Series of books on historical, literary, and scientific subjects, suitable for extension students and home-reading circles. Each volume is complete in itself, and the subjects are treated by competent writers in a broad and philosophic spirit. The volumes are suitably illustrated.

The Industrial History of England. By H. DE B. GIBBINS, Litt.D., M.A. Eighth Edition, Revised. With Maps and Plans. 3s.

A History of English Political Economy. By L. L. PRICE, M.A., Fellow of Oriel College, Oxon. Third Edition.

Problems of Poverty: An Inquiry into the Industrial Conditions of the Poor. By J. A. HOBSON, M.A. Fourth Edition.

Victorian Poets. By A. SHARP.

The French Revolution. By J. E. SYMES, M.A.

Psychology. By F. S. GRANGER, M.A. Second Edition.

The Evolution of Plant Life. By G. MASSEE.

Air and Water. By Prof. V. B. LEWES, M.A. Illustrated.

The Chemistry of Life and Health. By C. W. KIMMINS, M.A.

The Mechanics of Daily Life. By V. P. SELLS, M.A.

English Social Reformers. By H. DE B. GIBBINS, Litt.D.

English Trade and Finance in the Seventeenth Century. By W. A. S. HEWINS, B.A.

The Chemistry of Fire. By M. M. PATTISON MUIR, M.A.

A Text-Book of Agricultural Botany. By M. C. POTTER, M.A., F.L.S. Illustrated. Second Edition. 4s. 6d.

The Vault of Heaven. By R. A. GREGORY.

Meteorology. The Elements of Weather and Climate. By H. N. DICKSON, F.R.S.E., F.R.MET.SOC. Illustrated.

A Manual of Electrical Science. By G. J. BURCH, M.A., F.R.S. Illustrated. 3s.

The Earth: An Introduction to Physiography. By EVAN SMALL, M.A. Illustrated.

Insect Life. By F. W. THEOBALD, M.A. Illustrated.

English Poetry from Blake to Browning. By W. M. DIXON, M.A.

English Local Government. By E. JENKS, M.A.

The Greek View of Life. By G. L. DICKINSON. Second Edition.

Methuen's Junior School Books

EDITED BY OLIVER D. INSKIP, M.A., LL.D.,
HEADMASTER OF FRAMLINGHAM COLLEGE;

AND W. WILLIAMSON, B.A., F.R.S.L.,
HEADMASTER OF THE WEST KENT GRAMMAR SCHOOL, BROCKLEY.

Messrs. METHUEN are issuing under the above title a series of school class-books. These are adapted to the needs of the Lower and Middle Forms of Public Schools, and are suitable for the use of candidates preparing for the Oxford and Cambridge Junior Local Examinations. Each Volume is the work of a Master who has had considerable experience in teaching his subject; while special attention has been paid to the arrangement of the type and matter, which is as clear and concise as possible. The books contain numerous examination papers, and where the subject requires it are fully illustrated. In scholarship, in excellence of printing and lowness of price, this series will be found inferior to no other. The following are ready:—

A Class-Book of Dictation Passages. By W. WILLIAMSON, B.A. Sixth Edition. Crown 8vo, 1s. 6d.

In use at over three hundred Schools, including Bath College, Blackheath School, Bradfield College, Fauconberge School, Beccles; Cheltenham College, High School, Dublin; Edinburgh Academy, High School, Glasgow; Elizabeth College, Guernsey; Lancing College, Merchant Taylors' School, Mill Hill School, Nottingham High School, Owen's School, Islington; St. Olave's School, Southwark; St. Paul's School.

A Junior English Grammar. By W. WILLIAMSON, B.A. With numerous passages for Parsing and Analysis, and a Chapter on Essay-Writing. Crown 8vo, 240 pages, 2s.

A Junior Chemistry. By E. A. TYLER, B.A., F.C.S., Science Master at Swansea Grammar School. With 73 Illustrations. Crown 8vo, 2s. 6d.

The Gospel according to St. Mark. Edited by A. E. RUBIE, M.A., Headmaster of the Royal Naval School, Eltham. With Three Maps. Crown 8vo, 1s. 6d.

Adopted at Harrow, St. Paul's School, Bath College, Mill Hill School, Owen's School, Islington; King's College, Canterbury; Aravon School, Bray; Grammar School, Kirkby Ravensworth; Moorside School, Okehampton; Wellington College (Salop); Dronfield Grammar School, etc.

The Gospel according to St. Luke. Edited by W. WILLIAMSON, B.A.

The Acts of the Apostles. Edited by A. E. RUBIE, M.A.

A Junior French Grammar. By L. A. SORNET and M. J. ACATOS, Modern Language Masters at King Edward's School, Birmingham.

Several other volumes are in preparation.

PRINTED BY MORRISON AND GIBB LIMITED, EDINBURGH

Lightning Source UK Ltd.
Milton Keynes UK
UKOW07f0934040416

271488UK00010B/462/P